THE ROMANCE OF MISSIONARY HEROISM

True Stories of the Intrepid Bravery and Stirring Adventures of Missionaries with Primitive Peoples, Wild Animals and the Forces of Nature in All Parts of the World

VOLUME 2: AFRICA, THE AMERICAS, AND OCEANIA

WITH ILLUSTRATIONS

by
JOHN C. LAMBERT, M.A., D.D.

SCHMUL PUBLISHING COMPANY
NICHOLASVILLE, KENTUCKY

PUBLISHED 1979 BY SCHMUL PUBLISHING CO.

Churches and other noncommercial interests may reproduce portions of this book without prior written permission of the publisher, provided such quotations are not offered for sale—or other compensation in any form—whether alone or as part of another publication, and provided that the text does not exceed 500 words or five percent of the entire book, whichever is less, and does not include material quoted from another publisher. When reproducing text from this book, the following credit line must be included: "From *The Romance of Missionary Heroism Volume 2,* by John C. Lambert, 1979 by Schmul Publishing Co., Nicholasville, Kentucky. Used by permission."

This is a facsimile reprint of an important book that, due to the age of the original printing, may contain uneven lines, broken type, or other imperfections.

Cover image copyright: <a href="https://www.123rf.com/profile_turbodesign">turbodesign / 123RF Stock Photo</a>. Used by permission.

Cover image copyright: <a href='https://www.123rf.com/profile_deserttrends'>deserttrends</a>. Used by permission.

Published by Schmul Publishing Co.
PO Box 776
Nicholasville, KY 40340

Printed in the United States of America

ISBN 10: 0-88019-104-X
ISBN 13: 978-0-88019-104-3

Visit us on the Internet at www.wesleyanbooks.com, or order direct from the publisher by calling 800-772-6657, or by writing to the above address.

PREFATORY NOTE

THE author desires with much gratitude to acknowledge his debt to the following ladies and gentlemen, who have most kindly assisted him in gathering the materials for this book by giving their consent to his use of their writings, by lending him books and photographs, or in other ways:—

Miss Constance F. Gordon Cumming; the Rev. George Robson, D.D., Editor of the "Missionary Record of the United Free Church of Scotland"; the Rev. James Paton, D.D.; Mr. Fred S. Arnot, founder of the Garenganze Mission; the Picpus Fathers of the Damien Institute, Eccleshall; the Rev. E. P. Cachemaille, M.A., and Captain E. Poulden, R.N., the Secretaries of the South American Missionary Society; the Rev. J. W. Jack, M.A.; the Rev. W. MacNaughtan, M.A., of the Presbyterian Mission in Liao-Yang; Miss M. G. Cowan, Hon. Librarian of the Missionary Library at Lady Stair's House, Edinburgh; Mr. John Cochrane, of the Publications Office of the United Free Church; Mrs. D. R. MacKenzie, of the Livingstonia Mission, Lake Nyasa; Mr. R. K. Westwater.

He would also express his obligations to the following missionary societies and firms of publishers, which have most courteously allowed him to make use of the books mentioned in their proper places at the end of each chapter, and in some cases of illustrations of which they hold the copyright:—

The South American Society; The Religious Tract Society; The Society for Promoting Christian Knowledge; Messrs.

PREFATORY NOTE

Macmillan & Co.; The Clarendon Press; Messrs. Oliphant, Anderson, & Ferrier; The Fleming H. Revell Co.; Messrs. Hodder & Stoughton; Mr. T. Fisher Unwin; Messrs. S. W. Partridge & Co.; Messrs. Morgan & Scott; Messrs. Marshall Bros.; Messrs. Seeley & Co., Ltd.; The United Society of Christian Endeavour.

INTRODUCTION

IN a "foreword" which he contributes to Dr. Jacob Chamberlain's attractive missionary book, *In the Tiger Jungle,* Dr. Francis E. Clark expresses the opinion that one need not patronize sensational and unhealthy fiction to find stirring adventure and thrilling narrative, and then goes on to say:—

"There is one source which furnishes stories of intense and dramatic interest, abounding in novel situations and spiced with abundant adventure; and this source is at the same time the purest and most invigorating fountain at which our youth can drink. To change the figure, this is a mine hitherto largely unworked; it contains rich nuggets of ore, which will well repay the prospector in this new field."

The field to which Dr. Clark refers is the history of modern Christian missions. His meaning is that the adventurous and stirring side of missionary experience needs to be brought out, and emphasis laid upon the fact that the romantic days of missions are by no means past.

There are stories which are now among the classics of missionary romance. Such are the expedition of Hans Egede to Greenland, the lonely journeys of David Brainerd among the Indian tribes of the North American forests, the voyage of John Williams from one coral island of the Pacific to another in the little ship which his own hands had built, the exploration of the Dark Continent by David Livingstone in the hope of emancipating the black man's soul.

But among missionary lives which are more recent or less known, there are many not less noble or less thrilling than those just referred to; and the chapters which follow are an attempt to make this plain.

INTRODUCTION

There is, of course, a deeper side to Christian missions—a side that is essential and invariable—while the elements of adventure and romance are accidental and occasional. If in these pages the spiritual aspects of foreign mission work are but slightly touched upon, it is not because they are either forgotten or ignored, but simply because it was not part of the writer's present plan to deal with them. It is his hope, nevertheless, that some of those into whose hands this book may come will be induced by what they read to make fuller acquaintance with the lives and aims of our missionary heroes, and so will catch something of that spirit which led them to face innumerable dangers, toils, and trials among heathen and often savage peoples, whether in the frozen North or the burning South, whether in the hidden depths of some vast continent or among the scattered "islands of the ocean seas."

In the recently published *Memoirs of Archbishop Temple* we find the future Primate of the Church of England, when a youth of twenty, writing to tell his mother how his imagination had been stirred by the sight of Bishop Selwyn of New Zealand starting for the Pacific with a band of young men who had devoted themselves to the propagation of the Gospel among a benighted and barbarous people. "It is not mere momentary enthusiasm with me," he writes; "my heart beats whenever I think of it. I think it one of the noblest things England has done for a long time; almost the only thing really worthy of herself."

It is the author's earnest desire that the narratives which follow may help to kindle in some minds an enthusiasm for missions like that which characterized Frederick Temple to the very end of his long and strenuous life; or, better still, that they may even suggest to some who are looking forward to the future with a high ambition, and wondering how to make the most of life, whether there is any career which offers so many opportunities of romantic experience and heroic achievement as that of a Christian missionary.

CONTENTS

CHAPTER I

A TRAMP THROUGH THE GREAT PYGMY FOREST

PAGE

Pygmyland—Mr. A. B. Lloyd—From Uganda to the Congo mouth—The Great Forest—Vegetable and animal life—Gorillas—The elephant and the zareba—"Don't shoot; it's a man!"—The friendly Pygmies—Appearance and habits—Pygmy worship—The Ituri River—"Riding on a snake"—Down the Congo—Pygmyland and the Kingdom of Christ   13

AMERICA

CHAPTER II

AMONG THE INDIANS AND ESKIMO OF HUDSON BAY

A world of ice—The Hudson Bay ships—John Horden—A huge parish—Indians and Eskimo—Bishop of Moosonee—Ungava—"The last house in the world"—The tailless cow—Canoe adventures—The sea-ice—Last labours—*Si monumentum requiris*   29

CHAPTER III

THE "PRAYING-MASTER" OF THE REDSKINS

"The Apostle of the North"—The backwoods schoolmaster—Indians and fur-traders—At Norway House—The "praying-master"—R. M. Ballantyne—A famous dog-train—Camping in the snow—The Arctic night—The talking birch bark—A tragic incident—An Indian mother's forgiveness—Adopted by the Chippeways   42

CONTENTS

CHAPTER IV
IN THE LAND OF THE DAKOTAS
PAGE

Hiawatha—Stephen and Mary Riggs—The Sioux Indians—Indian *teepees*—"Eagle Help"—The scalping-party—A sad experience—The return of the bison—The Indian rising—A dreadful flight—The Dakota prisoners—Preaching in the prisoners' camp—A transformation on the prairies ... 60

CHAPTER V
IN THE FORESTS OF GUIANA

The Caribbean Islands—The Waraoons of the Orinoco—Kingsley's *At Last*—The tribes of Guiana—Rivers and *itabbos*—In the high woods—Swamps and forest bridges—Alligator and anaconda—The spotted jaguar—Humming-birds and fireflies, marabuntas and mosquitoes—The house in the palm tree—Legends and sorcerers—Cannibal mounds—A spiritual romance 74

CHAPTER VI
THE SAILOR MISSIONARY OF TIERRA DEL FUEGO

"The Neglected Continent"—The despised Fuegian—Darwin's testimony—Captain Allen Gardiner—South American Missionary Society—A sly Patagonian—An exploring expedition—The final enterprise—At Banner Cove—How the tragedy came about—The *cache* in the rocks—Spaniard Harbour—The end—Search and discovery—The diary—Victory through death 90

CHAPTER VII
THE SCHOONER OF KEPPEL ISLAND

A problem and a plan—The schooner—The island—Captain Gardiner's son—Jemmy Button—A disastrous enterprise—The massacre—Adventures of the ship's cook—Holding the fort—The new expedition—Forgiveness, not vengeance—Life on Keppel Island—The graves of the martyrs—Bishop Stirling and Ushuaia 106

CONTENTS

OCEANIA

CHAPTER VIII

THE MARTYR-BISHOP OF MELANESIA

PAGE

In the Eton playing-fields—A case of moral courage—Bishop Selwyn and Coley Patteson—Selwyn's work in Melanesia—Wanted a helper!—The helper found—Patteson as skipper and college tutor—As Bishop of Melanesia—Exciting adventures—The kidnappers—The Bishop's death 121

CHAPTER IX

ONE OF THE UNRETURNING BRAVE

An unexplored island—"Tamate"—Sea-dwellings and tree-dwellings—A ghastly parcel—Toeless feet—A perilous retreat—Dangers of the surf—Chalmers as a great explorer—As a teacher of the A B C —R. L. Stevenson and Tamate—The last expedition to the Fly River 136

CHAPTER X

FATHER DAMIEN OF MOLOKAI

The Hawaiian Islands—Captain Cook and Father Damien—A brave rescue—Molokai and its lepers—Under the pandanus tree—Doctor, undertaker, and grave digger—What was Father Damien like?—Himself a leper—In life and in death—A statue and a monument......................... 155

CHAPTER XI

AMONG THE CANNIBAL ISLANDS

The Fiji Islands—Man-eating—Human sacrifice—King George of Tonga—James Calvert—The King of Bau—The man-hunters—Two brave ladies—Murder of widows—King Thakombau and Queen Victoria—A happy Christian warrior   166

CONTENTS

CHAPTER XII

THE APOSTLE OF THE NEW HEBRIDES

PAGE

John Williams and John G. Paton—First night on Tanna—A lonely grave—The power of an empty revolver—Savages foiled by a retriever—A tragedy on Erromanga—The sandalwood traders—H.M.S. *Pelorus*—Bishop Selwyn's testimony—The power of prayer—"The last awful night"—Facing the cannibals—Jehovah's rain—Epilogue 179

CHAPTER XIII

KAPIOLANI AND THE GODDESS OF THE VOLCANO

Opukahaia at the gates of Yale—The expedition to Hawaii—Titus Coan—*New Acts of the Apostles*—An adventurous tour—Kapiolani—The march to the volcano—The pythoness of Pele—On the floor of the crater—The challenge to the fire-goddess—Sudden fall of the Hawaiian Dagons 194

LIST OF ILLUSTRATIONS

	PAGE
A Visit from the Pygmies	21
The Indian Chief Forgives His Enemy	48
Buffalo-Hunting in Winter	51
Shoeing Dogs in Northern Canada	54
A Red Indian Hunting Buffalo on Horseback	67
A Fight Between an Anaconda and an Alligator	82
Making Poisoned Arrows in the Guianas	85
Types of Patagonian Women	96
A Curious Patagonian Cradle	96
A Threatened Attack by Tierra Del Fuegians	107
Bishop Patteson Attacked at Santa Cruz	132
A Native Village in New Guinea	139
"I Walked Into That Eerie Place"	142
It Dazzled Him as a Bar of Gold Would Have a White Man"	145
New Guinea Lakatois or Rafts or Canoes	148
Dr. Paton Saved by His Dogs	183
"You Must Kill Me First	190
The Hawaiian Queen Defies the Goddess of the Volcano	203

CHAPTER I

A TRAMP THROUGH THE GREAT PYGMY FOREST

Pygmyland—Mr. A. B. Lloyd—From Uganda to the Congo mouth—The Great Forest—Vegetable and animal life—Gorillas—The elephant and the zareba—"Don't shoot; it's a man!"—The friendly Pygmies—Appearance and habits—Pygmy worship—The Ituri River—"Riding on a snake"—Down the Congo—Pygmyland and the Kingdom of Christ.

OF Stanley's different expeditions to Africa the greatest, though in some respects the least successful, was the last, when he marched by way of the Congo for the relief of Emin Pasha. And of all the thrilling chapters of *In Darkest Africa*, where he tells the story of that long struggle against frightful difficulties, none are more fascinating than those in which he describes his march through the vast primeval forest of the Upper Congo and its tributary, the Aruwimi, and his encounters with the strange dwarfish people who dwell in that region of interminable gloom. Rumours of the Pygmies had come to the civilized world from time to time, especially through the reports of Arab traders; but few persons believed those rumours to have much more reality behind them than the tales of Baron Münchausen. Stanley proved, however, that the existence of the Pygmies

MR. A. B. LLOYD

was a fact and not a fable. And it was natural that a later traveller, who, in addition to Stanley's courage and love of adventure, possessed a large share of the missionary spirit, should visit the Great Forest with the view of learning something about the religion of the Pygmy folk, and particularly of seeing what prospect there might be of carrying the light of Christian civilization with success into that shadowy world in which this unknown people lived and died.

Mr. A. B. Lloyd, the hero of this enterprise, was a young missionary of the C.M.S. who had been working for some time in the district of Toro on the western side of the Uganda Protectorate, under the very shadow of the giant snow-capped peaks of Ruwenzori, anciently known as the Mountains of the Moon. His experiences already had been of an exciting kind, for he had been in the thick of the fighting in Uganda during the year 1897, when the Soudanese troops mutinied, and Mwanga, the dethroned king, himself raised the standard of rebellion against the British rule. Primarily Mr. Lloyd's duties in the campaign had been to act as interpreter to the British forces and to give the wounded the benefit of such surgical skill as he possessed. But he was a good shot with a Martini rifle, and a "handy man" generally, who could work a Maxim gun in case of need. He did not hesitate, accordingly, as a loyal British subject, to play his part like a soldier in the suppression of the rebellion, along with the handful of white men who at that time represented Queen Victoria and the British flag in the heart of Africa. His companion and friend, the Rev. G. Pilkington, fell in the course of the fighting, and Mr. Lloyd himself had several

UGANDA TO THE CONGO MOUTH

narrow escapes in the eleven engagements in which he took part. At last, after a long period of great strain, a reaction came, and he was laid down with malarial fever. On recovering from the attack he was ordered to give up his work for a time and leave for England in order to recruit.

In these circumstances ninety-nine men out of a hundred would have made for home from Uganda by the ordinary East Coast route, via Zanzibar. But Mr. Lloyd was the hundredth man, and he decided to strike westwards right across the continent, by way of the Pygmy Forest of the Upper Aruwimi. His preparations were soon made, for unlike Stanley he had no intention of advancing at the head of a small army. He secured as a guide a man who had once before passed through the forest; furnished himself with provisions for three months; gathered a few porters; and with a bicycle, a camera, a donkey, and a faithful little dog named Sally, set out upon his tramp into the unknown.

For the first stages of the journey the way was plain. The mighty mass of Ruwenzori, which barred direct progress to the west, had to be circumvented, and thereafter the route lay through a charming plain abounding in game, where to the delight of his followers Mr. Lloyd was able to supply them plentifully with elephant steak and antelope joints. After five or six days' pleasant marching a river was crossed which forms the boundary between the Uganda Protectorate and the Congo Free State, and four days' progress through King Leopold's territory brought the party to a Belgian fort called Mbeni, where they rested for two days. Here they saw running along the

VEGETABLE AND ANIMAL LIFE

western horizon a long dark belt which, they were told, was the commencement of the Great Forest. Leaving Mbeni they made for the centre of this black line, and soon plunged into a mysterious region of darkness and solitude from which they were not to escape for many days.

The Great Forest of the Congo has an area of no less than 300,000 square miles—about six times the area of England not including Wales. The scenery which meets the traveller's eye is described by Mr. Lloyd as possessed of a beauty of its own—a beauty that is thoroughly weird and uncanny. Majestic trees tower up towards the sky to the height often of 200 feet, interlacing their foliage so closely that not even the rays of the tropical sun are able to pierce through the dense barrier. The day at best is a dull twilight, while at night a blackness falls which might almost be described as solid. In spite of the want of sunshine, however, the vegetable life is wondrously profuse. Strange ferns and flowers spring on every hand, and gigantic creepers, with cables which are sometimes a foot in diameter, climb up the trunks and along the branches from tree to tree until the whole forest becomes a confused tangle of luxuriant growths.

The animal life is not less exuberant. Insects swarm and chirp and buzz on every hand. Birds of the most variegated plumage flit from bough to bough, some of them uttering deep musical sounds like the tolling of a bell, others of the parrot tribe whose only music is the harshest of screams. And there are other denizens of this vast woodland. "Elephants and buffalo are met with constantly, sometimes in herds, sometimes singly; wild pigs and forest antelope, many species of gazelles,

GORILLAS

chimpanzee, gorilla, and vast quantities of monkeys of every kind are seen; leopards, panthers, wild cats, civets, hyenas, and reptiles. Deadly snakes will be found hanging from the branches of the trees, or curled up amongst the decaying vegetation beneath; huge black adders, pythons, bright green snakes with wicked red eyes, whipcord snakes which look for all the world like green twigs. The forest is threaded with a network of rivers and streams, and all seemed full of fish. There are also crocodiles and hippos, water-snakes and lizards, leeches and slow-worms."

With the great majority of these animals the traveller was quite familiar, for, by the necessity of his calling, a pioneer missionary in Central Africa is something of a sportsman, since the very life of his followers and himself when on the march may depend on his skill in shooting game. Elephants, buffaloes, and antelopes he had often dealt with. The roar of the lion and the yelp of the leopard in search of its prey were familiar sounds to his ears. But he had not long entered the forest when evidence came of the near presence of the gorilla, an animal which is only to be found in Central Africa, and there only in the depths of "the forest primeval."

They had reached a particularly dark bit of the forest where no light at all seemed to come from the sky, so that, though it was only one p.m., a gloom as of night was all about them. Suddenly they heard a strange noise not far off, as of deep voices angrily quarrelling. For a moment every one was scared, but the guide assured them that it was nothing else than *nkima nkubwa* ("big monkeys"). The Belgians at Fort Mbeni had told

DIFFICULTIES OF THE MARCH

Mr. Lloyd that he would probably meet with gorillas, and gorillas these doubtless were. But for the present he was quite content with hearing their voices, having no desire at the head of his unarmed porters to make their closer acquaintance.

For six days the little expedition fought its way through wood and jungle without meeting with any adventures of an especially thrilling kind. Every day, however, the difficulties of steady progress grew greater. The undergrowth seemed to get thicker and thicker as they advanced, and Mr. Lloyd had to walk in front of the line with an old sword-bayonet, chopping a way for himself and for the porters who followed with the loads. The guide, too, it soon turned out, was hopelessly at sea as to direction; and so Mr. Lloyd had further to pilot his company as best he could with the help of a compass, trying to keep a north-westerly course with the view of striking the Ituri river, a principal affluent of the Aruwimi, and then of proceeding along its banks until they should emerge from the forest. Besides overcoming the obstacles presented by the tangles of bush and creeper, the caravan had every now and then to cross one or other of the numerous marshy streams which find their way through the forest, most of them being deep enough to take a man up to the armpits, and some of them so polluted with rotting vegetation as to be highly offensive to the smell.

A day's march under such conditions was very exhausting; but the work of the day was far from over when the day's tramp was done. A piece of ground had to be cleared where a tent could be pitched, and a strong

"DON'T SHOOT; IT'S A MAN!"

zareba or fence built round it as a protection against wild animals—leopards, panthers, and elephants—which gave the travellers many an uneasy moment. Through the night they often heard elephants squealing loudly, and trampling through the bush in the immediate neighbourhood of their little camp. And one morning when Mr. Lloyd had risen early and gone out of the tent before any of his men were awake, he found a huge old tusker with its head over the zareba, "evidently in deep thought, and wondering what on earth this could mean."

Six days had passed since entering the forest, and not a trace of the Pygmies had anywhere been seen. Mr. Lloyd began to wonder if the Pygmy stories were really true. But on the seventh day, as he was walking in advance of the caravan, rifle in hand, accompanied by his black boy and looking out for a shot at some wild pigs which had been sighted shortly before, the boy stopped of a sudden, cried, "Monkey!" and pointed towards the top of a high cotton-tree beneath which they were passing. Mr. Lloyd looked up, and there sure enough was a creature which from its size he took to be a gorilla. Now his men had been glad to eat monkey-meat before this when nothing better was to be had. So he raised his rifle to his shoulder, took careful aim, and was in the act of pulling the trigger when his boy hastily pulled his arm and exclaimed, "Don't shoot—it's a man!" At once he saw that the boy was right. It was a strongly built little man, who, seeing that he was observed, ran along the branch on which he stood, and jumping from tree to tree with the agility of a monkey, soon disappeared in the depths of the forest.

THE FRIENDLY PYGMIES

They had pitched their tent that same afternoon, and Mr. Lloyd had sat down at the tent door with a book in his hand intending to read for a little, when on looking up, he saw a number of little faces peering at him through the thickets in front, and one in particular, which was nearer than the rest, peeping round the trunk of a huge tree that grew right opposite. The boys, who were cooking food for the evening meal, noticed the little people at the same time and sprang up in alarm, for they knew the Pygmies only by report, and thought of them as a kind of devils. For some time the white man and the dwarfs remained motionless, gazing silently at one another in a mutual fascination, though Mr. Lloyd felt all the while that at any moment he might be transfixed with a shower of poisoned arrows from the bows with which the Pygmies were armed. Stanley had characterized them as " malicious dwarfs," and his warlike company had been greatly harassed by them again and again. But at length it occurred to the missionary, still sitting peacefully in his camp-chair, to call out the ordinary salutation of the people of Toro; and when he did so, to his great surprise, one little man immediately returned the greeting in the same language. He then said, "Come here and let us talk together"; and, very shyly, the nearest of the dwarfs crept forwards, followed by a few of the others, half covering his face with his hand and staring through his fingers at the white man in a sort of amazement.

As the Pygmies approached, Mr. Lloyd was struck first of all by their extreme shortness of stature, four feet being the average height of a full-grown man, but next

A VISIT FROM THE DWARFS

I called out, "Come and let us talk together." First one man came creeping towards me, then some of his companions who dodged behind one another. They were all short (about 4 feet) but powerfully built, with broad chests and well-developed muscles. I chatted away to the chief, who was the first to approach me. He knew the Toro language, and amazed me with his smart answers.

A GOOD-NATURED CHIEF

by their exceedingly well-knit figures and powerful limbs. The one who replied to his salutation turned out to be the chief of the party. This man had once come in contact with some people from Toro, and hence knew a little of the Toro language. With him, Mr. Lloyd was able to carry on an imperfect conversation, in which he learned something of the Pygmies and their ways. One of the first things the chief told him was, that for six days he and his people had been following the caravan and keeping it under constant observation. "But we never saw you," the traveller objected. Whereupon the little man laughed with great glee, accepting this as a high compliment to the forest-craft of himself and his followers. During the whole of that time the Pygmies had the caravan entirely in their power; but the very smallness of the company and the evident peacefulness of its intentions had disarmed their suspicions. Mr. Lloyd's experience in the forest, so different from Stanley's, showed that the dwarfs are by no means so "malicious" as that great explorer imagined. And his testimony, like that of Dr. Livingstone or Mr. Joseph Thomson, points to the conclusion that where no warlike demonstrations are made, the African savage of whatsoever tribe is in ordinary circumstances a good-natured fellow, who is ready to give the right hand of fellowship to those who show themselves peaceful and friendly.

With the Pygmies Mr. Lloyd struck up a friendship on the spot. The chief testified to his goodwill by presenting him with an antelope he had just killed, and also with a pot of wild honey, of which great quantities are gathered by these people from the hollows of the trees. That

APPEARANCE AND HABITS

night the two parties encamped in the forest side by side, and they parted next morning on the best of terms, after Mr. Lloyd had made several ineffectual efforts to obtain photographs of the strangers. He found that snapshots were impossible in the forest twilight, while the Pygmies were too restless to submit to time exposures. And so, after spoiling about a dozen plates, he had to give up the idea in despair.

After this, different parties of Pygmies were met with at various times in the further course of the march through the forest, some of whom even brought their women to see the white traveller. The women were comely little creatures, averaging 3 feet 10 inches in height, with light tan-coloured skin. Like Stanley, Mr. Lloyd was much struck by the beautiful eyes of the Pygmy women. These are singularly large and lustrous, but so quick and restless that they never seem to fix their gaze upon any object for one second at a time.

The Pygmies are essentially a wandering people. They never think of clearing the ground and cultivating the soil, and are content to wander from place to place, gathering the honey which the bees have stored and the fruit and beans and nuts which grow plentifully on the trees, but above all living on the spoils of the chase. They are fearless and expert hunters, who do not hesitate with their little bows and arrows to attack the largest elephants. Sometimes they have to follow one of these forest monsters for days, and shoot hundreds of arrows into it before it falls down and dies from exhaustion and loss of blood. Then they camp around it and feast upon its flesh day after day. When nothing but the hide and

THE ITURI RIVER

skeleton are left, they seize their weapons once more and go forth in search of another quarry.

Particularly interesting to this traveller were the evidences he discovered of the Pygmy worship. It has sometimes been alleged that these Congo dwarfs have no religion; but Mr. Lloyd had abundant evidence that this was not the case. Sometimes at the foot of a huge tree there might be seen a bundle of food neatly tied up in a piece of bark cloth, or a pot of honey, or a humble offering of forest beans. The Pygmies venerate the Spirit of their forest home, and look upon a giant tree as enshrining that Spirit's presence. And besides their tree shrines Mr. Lloyd came upon temples of their own building—little huts, roughly fenced in from the forest, and hardly better than the tiny shelters of boughs and leaves in which they lie down at night, but holy places in their eyes, because there they deposit the gifts they wish to offer to the invisible Spirit of the woods.

Having successfully struck the river Ituri, the expedition made its way along the banks, and at length issued from the forest at a place called Avakubi, where there was a Belgian station with an officer in command. Here the white traveller was kindly received, and stayed for two days, thoroughly enjoying the comforts of civilized life after all the privations of camp arrangements in the Pygmy Forest. And now it was a comfort to think that though he had still some 1500 miles of African travel to face, no more tramping would be necessary. Fifteen days' paddling in a canoe down the Aruwimi would bring him to the Congo. Reaching that great river, he would connect with a service of steamers running between Stanley

THE BANGWA

Falls and Leopoldville. At the latter place a passage would be secured by another steamer to Boma, at the Congo mouth, and from that place the Belgian mail boat would carry him homewards.

This was a comparatively tame programme for one who had just fought his way for weeks through all the dangers and terrors of the Great Forest; and yet the journey, especially in its earlier stages, was full of interest, and not without adventure. More than once the canoe came to grief in shooting the rapids, for African boatmen are not such experts at this kind of work as the North American Indians; and once at least Mr. Lloyd was all but drowned. Moreover, the Aruwimi for a long distance runs through a country in which cannibalism is practised almost as a fine art by a bold and warlike race known as the Bangwa. More than once on landing at a Bangwa village Mr Lloyd had to face a trying experience. A crowd of tall savages, each with a cruel-looking knife shaped like a sickle, walked round him, looking him up and down, as if taking stock of his condition and considering whether he was worth killing. The trial was all the more unpleasant that he knew perfectly well how those same execution knives were used. When about to hold a cannibal feast, the Bangwa lead a captive beneath a tree, and bending down a large bough fasten his neck to it. One swish of the keen sickle-knife severs the neck completely, and the bough, springing back to its original position, tosses the poor head with a kind of derision high into the air.

Apart from disagreeable sensations on his own private account, Mr. Lloyd often had to witness scenes which were horrible and sickening. It was a common thing to

RIDING ON A SNAKE"

see a group of men sitting round a fire and eagerly watching the leg of a man that was being roasted, and next falling upon it and devouring it with unconcealed gusto. The visitor found, however, that the cannibalism of the Bangwa was not simply a depraved appetite, but in large part the result of superstition. They firmly believed that the spirit of the dead warrior passes into the body of the man who eats him, so that by partaking of the flesh of his slain foe a man will increase his own strength and courage. It is in keeping with this that a woman is seldom, if ever, eaten by the Bangwa.

The donkey with which Mr. Lloyd started from Toro not only proved to be of no use as a steed, but was a source of infinite trouble through her habit of floundering into swamps and sticking fast in the bush on every possible occasion, and he was glad to sell her on the first opportunity. His little dog Sally, after many exciting adventures and hairbreadth escapes, came to an untimely end in the jaws of a crocodile. But his bicycle, which had been carried safely through the forest in sections, he was now able to put together again, and one day in a large Bangwa community inhabited by some thousands of people he appeared suddenly in the village street pedalling along at the top of his speed. The sensation he produced was enormous. The cannibals rushed about in consternation, knocking each other down in their eagerness to get out of the way, and crying, "The white man is riding on a snake." By and by he dismounted, and calling to the chief, tried to persuade him to come and examine this strange flying creature. But his assurances that it was perfectly harmless were of no avail. The

PYGMYLAND

cannibal declined to come any nearer, saying, as he pointed to the long trail left by the wheels on the village street, that he always knew a snake's track when he saw it.

The intrepid traveller reached Boma safely at last, and caught the mail steamer for Europe. He had suffered many hardships, but he had also had not a few experiences that were pleasant—especially in the retrospect. And not the least pleasing of his impressions was the conviction which had grown upon him day by day, whether in the forest of the Pygmies or among the cannibals of the Aruwimi river, that great as was the darkness in which those people lived, they had many fine characteristics of their own, and offered a fresh and splendid field for the messengers of the Christian Gospel.

The rapidity of his march, combined with his complete ignorance of the languages of the Congo region, so different from those of Uganda, made it impossible for Mr. Lloyd to engage during his journey in any kind of Christian work among the natives. But it was a missionary purpose which carried him through the Dark Forest, and that missionary purpose had not been fruitless.

The C.M.S., it is true, has not hitherto felt justified in taking up work among the Pygmies. But Mr. Lloyd may be said to have claimed that strange people for Christ. Stanley had shown that, so far from being on the plane almost of the brute creation, they were a people of a quick intelligence. Mr. Lloyd proved that they were also possessed of religious ideas which offer a foundation for a higher faith and worship than their own. An American missionary traveller, the Rev. Mr. Geil, has followed in Mr. Lloyd's steps by traversing the forest, and has added

AND THE KINGDOM OF CHRIST

something further to our knowledge of its very interesting inhabitants. There is every reason to hope that Pygmyland, like many another part of the Dark Continent, will one day be brought into the Kingdom of Christ.

NOTE.—The book which contains Mr. Lloyd's narrative of his remarkable journey is entitled *In Dwarf Land and Cannibal Country*, and is published by Mr. T. Fisher Unwin. The present author has to thank Mr. Unwin for his kind permission to make use of Mr. Lloyd's narrative.

AMERICA

CHAPTER II

AMONG THE INDIANS AND ESKIMO OF HUDSON BAY

A world of ice—The Hudson Bay ships—John Horden—A huge parish—Indians and Eskimo—Bishop of Moosonee—Ungava—" The last house in the world "—The tailless cow—Canoe adventures—The sea-ice—Last labours—*Si monumentum requiris.*

TO those who as boys have read Mr. R. M. Ballantyne's *Ungava* and *Young Fur Traders*, the name of Hudson Bay will always suggest a world of glorious adventure and romance. They have visions of Indians shooting swift rapids in their bark canoes, or of Eskimo on an ice-floe fighting a fierce polar bear or lying in wait for an unwary seal. They see the trapper on a winter morning, with his gun on his shoulder, skimming lightly on broad snowshoes over the powdery snow, as he goes his rounds from one trap to another through a forest which has been transformed by icicle and snowflake into a wonderland of magical beauty. Or they remember the traders in a lonely fort, doing their best to keep their hearts jolly and their noses free from frostbite, at a time when the thermometer is fifty degrees below zero, and the

THE HUDSON BAY SHIPS

pen cannot be dipped into the ink-bottle because the ink has turned into a solid lump of ice.

The present writer has a vivid recollection of a sunny midsummer season spent in the Orkneys. In Stromness harbour he saw some strongly built but old-fashioned vessels preparing to set sail, and felt an almost boyish thrill of delight as he learned that these were the Hudson Bay ships about to start on their annual voyage for the coasts of Labrador, from what is their last port of call in the British Isles. He thought of that solitary route, where sometimes never a sail is sighted from one side of the Atlantic to another. And he remembered that, though the bright summer sun might be shining on our islands, these ships would have to struggle with many a bristling iceberg before they could discharge at Moose Fort or York Factory the precious cargo on which depended the comfort and even the lives of those who held the outposts of the British Empire along the frontiers of the Frozen North.

Let us go back to the year 1851, and imagine ourselves on board of a stout old wooden ship of the whaler type, which has fought its way from Stromness across the North Atlantic and through the floes and bergs of Hudson Straits, and is now entering the wide expanse of Hudson Bay itself. She is squarely built, and armed at her bows with thick blocks of timber called ice-chocks, to enable her to do daily battle with the floating ice. On board of her as passengers are a young Englishman named John Horden and his wife. Horden is a teacher who is being sent out from England by the Church Missionary Society to try to bring some Christian light into the minds and

JOHN HORDEN

hearts of the Indians and Eskimo scattered round the shores of this great inland sea. The vessel is nearing her destination, but the danger is not yet over; indeed the worst dangers are yet to come. Horden himself describes their experiences:—

" Ahead, stretching as far as the eye could reach, is ice—ice; now we are in it. More and more difficult becomes the navigation. We are at a standstill. We go to the mast-head—ice; rugged ice in every direction! One day passes by—two, three, or four. The cold is intense. Our hopes sink lower and lower; a week passes. The sailors are allowed to get out and have a game at football; the days pass on; for nearly three weeks we are imprisoned. Then there is a movement in the ice. It is opening. The ship is clear! Every man is on deck. Up with the sails in all speed! Crack, crack, go the blows from the ice through which we are passing; but we shall now soon be free, and in the open sea. Ah! no prisoner ever left his prison with greater joy than we left ours."

A few days after, the voyagers reached Moose Fort, at the extreme south-west corner of Hudson Bay, and the young teacher found himself on the spot which was to be his home for the rest of his life.

And now let us look at the task which lay before him. When John Wesley said that he took the whole world for his parish, he was speaking figuratively; but this inexperienced young man found himself literally responsible for the educational and religious welfare of a district 1500 miles long by 1500 broad. Indeed, lengthwise his parish stretched out indefinitely into space, for though bounded on the south by the settled parts of Canada, it

A HUGE PARISH

might be said to extend in the opposite direction right up to the North Pole. Within this huge area, and planted along the coasts of Hudson Bay, a few trading posts of the Hudson Bay Company were scattered, several hundred miles apart. And here and there small bands of Indians and Eskimo were settled, who gained a precarious livelihood by hunting and fishing. Apart from those who lived in the neighbourhood of Moose Fort, or visited it from time to time to barter skins and furs for English goods, Horden could reach the people of this vast territory only by toilsome and dangerous journeys, performed in summer in a bark canoe, and in winter on snow-shoes or in a sledge drawn by a team of Eskimo dogs.

First of all, however, he had to learn something of the language, or rather of the languages, for there were several of them. Around Moose Fort the Indians were Crees, but in other parts of the country there were Ojjibeways and Chippeways, each of whom spoke an entirely different dialect. Farther north, on both sides of the Bay, were the Eskimo, whose speech bore no resemblance to any of the Indian tongues. The language difficulties did not trouble Horden very seriously. Most Europeans are greatly puzzled by the peculiarities of the agglutinative family of languages used by the native tribes of North America. But though Horden confessed that Cree was a jaw-breaking speech, and that Greek and Latin in comparison were tame affairs, he had so much determination, combined with such a knack for picking up new words and forms of expression, that in a very few months he was able to preach to the people without the help of an interpreter. He made mistakes, of course. Once he

ARDUOUS EXPEDITIONS

was speaking of the creation of Adam and Eve. All went well till he came to describe Eve's manner of coming into the world, when he observed that his hearers were "smiling audibly." He found that instead of saying that the woman was made "out of one of Adam's ribs," he had said "out of one of Adam's pipes." *Ospikakun* is "his rib," and *ospwakun* "his pipe." But by and by he was able to speak with correctness as well as fluency, not in one language, but in several. And having taught the people to read, and himself learned how to work a printing-press, he scattered abroad thousands of Gospels and other books which he had translated into the various tongues.

Mr. Horden showed such aptness for his work that before long he was ordained as a clergyman by the nearest bishop—the Bishop of Rupert's Land, who had to make for this purpose a journey of six weeks, mostly by canoe. And now Horden himself began to make those constant and arduous expeditions to all parts of the territory which form the most striking feature of the story of his life. "Arduous," his biographer says, "is but a mild expression for the troubles, trials, privations, and tremendous difficulties attendant on travel through the immense trackless wastes lying between many of the posts —wastes intersected by rivers and rapids, varied only by tracts of pathless forest swept by fierce storms."

Sometimes he went on from day to day for four or five hundred miles, without ever seeing tent or house or even the trace of a human being by the way. Often he encountered men who delighted in bloodshed, and thought little of killing and eating their fellow-creatures when other means of subsistence failed. Once he met an Indian who during

UNGAVA

the preceding winter had murdered and devoured, one after another, his whole family of six children, in order to satisfy the cravings of hunger. As for his own food on these journeys, he was obliged to take whatever he could get. "I have eaten," he says, "white bear, black bear, wild cat; while for a week or ten days I have had nothing but beaver, and glad indeed I have been to get it."

Let us follow him to some of his more distant stations, and see what he found there, or how he fared by the way. First, however, let the fact be mentioned that, after twenty years of remarkably successful labour, he was summoned to England to be consecrated in Westminster Abbey as Bishop of Moosonee, the name given to the new diocese, of which Moose Fort was the strategic centre. His elevation in rank and dignity made little difference in the nature of his ordinary occupations, and so, in describing some of the incidents of his tours, we shall take these without distinction from the earlier or the later period of his life.

Far up the eastern side of Hudson Bay lies the region of Ungava, with the Little Whale and Great Whale rivers flowing through it to the sea. For the Eskimo of this district Horden always had a special affection and regard. He loved his Indian flock too; but he found these Eskimo more responsive, more eager to learn, and more teachable in every way. Bleak and desolate as the country was around Moose, it was colder and wilder still towards Ungava, where from year's end to year's end the snow never entirely disappeared, and the white bear of the floes took the place of the black bear of the forest. In summer the Eskimo lived in tents made of sealskins; but in winter, like their Greenland cousins, in houses built of slabs of

"LAST HOUSE IN THE WORLD"

frozen snow. Bears and seals were hunted in winter, but in summer there came the fiercer excitements of a great whale drive. The whales would come over the river bars in vast numbers, and then every kayak was afloat, and with harpoon and line the eager sportsmen followed their prey to the death. On one occasion Mr. Horden himself took part in a whale fishery in which no fewer than a thousand prizes were secured—a world of wealth and feasting to the poor Eskimo.

But no matter what the Eskimo were about, if they heard that the white teacher had come they dropped spear and harpoon, and trotted off to listen, to sing, and to pray, in a fashion which showed how deeply interested they were. By and by Bishop Horden was able to obtain for them a missionary of their own, who settled on the spot, and under whose teaching the whole colony around the Whale River region became not only thoroughly civilized, but earnestly Christian.

Still farther north than Ungava, but on the opposite side of Hudson Bay, is a station called Fort Churchill. Horden dubbed it "the last house in the world," for there was no other between it and the North Pole. There the cold in winter is as intense almost as in any spot on the surface of the globe. The diary of an expedition to this lonely outpost, undertaken in the depth of winter, is specially interesting. Horden travelled in a cariole, or dog sledge, accompanied by Indian guides. The temperature was never less than thirty, and sometimes nearly fifty degrees below zero. The greatest precautions had to be taken against frostbite. Every evening, when they encamped in the forest, about an hour and a half was spent

A HETEROGENEOUS POPULATION

in erecting a thick, high barricade of pine branches as a protection against the piercing wind. An enormous fire was also necessary, for one of ordinary size would have made little impression on the frozen air. When a hearty supper had been cooked and eaten, and the Indians had lighted their pipes, the little company would sit around the blazing pine-logs and tell of hunting adventures, or of hairbreadth escapes from the perils of the forest and the flood. As bedtime drew near, all joined earnestly in a short service of praise and prayer, and then lay down to sleep under the open sky, which glittered with frosty stars, or glowed and throbbed with the streaming rays of the brilliant Northern Lights.

Though the last house in the world, Fort Churchill had a heterogeneous population of English traders, Indians, and Eskimo. The Eskimo of the west were a fiercer people than those on the eastern side of the great bay, and were much feared even by the Chippeway Indians—themselves dangerous customers to deal with. Often an Eskimo would come to the station with his face marked with red ochre, a sign that he had recently committed a murder. This red mark was their peculiar glory, for while they prided themselves on their prowess in killing a walrus or a polar bear, they thought it a much higher honour to have slain a human being. Churchill was thus a very needful field of operations in the eyes of the Bishop, and Horden did not rest until he had planted a church there, with a minister of its own to attend to the wants of the variegated flock.

In spite of its rigours and occasional tragedies, life at Churchill was not without its own small humours too. Horden was fond of telling his friends farther south about

THE TAILLESS COW

the Churchill cows. There were three of them. The first was a dwarf. The second was so lean and supple that she could milk herself with her own mouth, and was therefore condemned to go in harness, carrying a bag round her udder which effectually prevented her from enjoying a drink of fresh milk whenever she pleased. The third member of the dairy had been despoiled of her tail one winter night by some hungry wolves. The result was that when summer came and the flies began to swarm—and in the brief, hot summer they *do* swarm around Hudson Bay —they threatened to eat up all of her that the wolves had left; for without a tail she was perfectly helpless against their assaults. But an ingenious trader bethought himself of a dead cow's tail which was lying in the store:—

"Why not use that? The suggestion was at once acted upon; the tail was attached to the stump by means of some twine, and over it was tied some canvas, well saturated with Stockholm tar. It was a great success, and the creature was again able to do battle with her diminutive but persevering foes."

In the course of his constant journeys in such a land, Bishop Horden, as will readily be imagined, had many a narrow escape. Shooting the rapids in a bark canoe is one of the most exhilarating of experiences, but sometimes one of the most dangerous. Horden, who travelled thousands of miles by water almost every year, had full taste of the dangers. Once a large canoe in which he was ascending a swollen river was caught in a strong current and dragged down towards some difficult rapids, while the Indians, with faces upstream, dug their paddles into the water and strained their muscles nearly to the bursting-

THE SEA-ICE

point. Their efforts, however, were quite fruitless. The canoe went back and back, and at length was swept at lightning speed into the boiling flood. Fortunately the crew were equal to the emergency. In a moment they all turned swiftly round in their places, thus converting what had been the stern into the bow, and by careful steering through the rocks the canoe shot safely out at last into the smooth water beneath the rapids.

On another occasion, a smaller canoe struck with a heavy crash upon a rock right in mid-stream. A great hole was made, and the water came pouring in. But by great exertions the canoe was brought to shore before it had time to sink; and in an hour or two it was sufficiently patched up again. For if an Indian canoe is easily damaged, it is easily repaired.

"One goes to a birch tree and cuts off a large piece of bark, another digs up some roots and splits them, a third prepares some pitch, and in the course of an hour or two the bark is sewn into the bottom of the canoe, the seams are covered with pitch, and we are once more loading our little vessel."

But the narrowest escape that Horden ever made was connected with the sudden break-up of the sea-ice. They were crossing a frozen inlet on the south of Hudson Bay, when the cold season was rather far advanced for a short cut of this kind to be altogether prudent. Just in the middle, when they were about ten miles from the nearest point of land, the guide gave a sudden exclamation and pointed seawards. As they looked, they saw mass after mass of ice rise up and fall back into the sea; and they knew that, with the approach of the warmer weather, the

TRIALS AND ANXIETIES

solid surface was going to pieces before an incoming tide. The guide next struck his stick sharply on the spot on which they stood, and the stick went clean through. Every one knew what that meant—the ice was quite rotten. "Get into the cariole at once!" the guide cried to Mr. Horden. The Bishop jumped in, but his weight forced the hinder part of the sledge downwards into the sea. Both sledge and occupant might have disappeared in a moment if it had not been for the prompt action of the sagacious dogs. They seemed to realize at once Horden's danger and their own. Straining on their harness, they quickly drew the cariole out of its terrible position, and made for the nearest shore at full gallop, while the Indians ran behind not less swiftly. Eskimo dogs and Indians are both good long-distance runners, and we are not surprised to be told that neither men nor dogs ever thought of halting until they felt the solid ground once more beneath their feet.

There were many trials and anxieties, as well as dangers, in Bishop Horden's life. Once the annual ship from England, so eagerly expected, was wrecked on a reef, and a large part of the provisions and other goods on which both traders and missionaries depended to carry them through another twelvemonth was utterly lost. Sometimes there came a bad season—no game in the forest, no wild geese for the goose-hunters along the shore—and the poor Indians died by the dozen. Above all, there was the great trial of parting from his wife and children, for Mrs. Horden, his faithful companion and helpmate from the very first, had to take the boys and girls to England to receive their education. But the good Bishop never

"SI MONUMENTUM REQUIRIS"

lost his cheerfulness or relaxed his activity. He was true always to the motto of his life: "*The happiest man is he who is most diligently employed about his Master's business.*"

Even on his death-bed his diligence did not cease. His last letter, dictated when he was no longer able to write himself, shows him, like Bede in the well-known narrative of his pupil Cuthbert, busy to the last with the task of New Testament translation. He suffered dreadful torture from rheumatism, the natural result of forty-two years of "roughing it" in a climate where the temperature varies from 100 degrees in the shade at the height of the brief summer to 50 degrees below zero in the depth of winter. But in the intervals between the sharp attacks of almost intolerable pain, he pushed eagerly on with a revised version of the New Testament in the Cree language: "Picture me in my work," he writes to his friends in England. "I am lying on my back in my bed, Mr. Richards is sitting at a table by my side. I have my English Bible, the Revised Version, in my hand; Mr. Richards has my translation before him, which he is reading to me slowly and distinctly. Every sentence is very carefully weighed, and all errors are corrected. This is a glorious occupation, and I cannot feel too thankful that I am able to follow it in these days of my weakness."

The end came suddenly, but it did not come too soon. Horden had accomplished his task, and left behind him a splendid record of heroic work heroically done. *Si monumentum requiris, circumspice,* is Sir Christopher Wren's appropriate epitaph in St. Paul's Cathedral.

RESULTS OF MINISTRY

John Horden's monument is to be seen in the presence of a pervasive Christian civilization all around the shores of Hudson Bay. When he went there first, he found the people living for the most part under the cruel spell of their conjurers. It was a common thing to strangle the sick with a bowstring in order to save further trouble. Aged parents were got rid of in the same way to avoid the expense of supporting them. Murder for gain was rife on every hand. When Bishop Horden died, a complete change had passed over the great part of the Hudson Bay region. More than one Indian had been educated and ordained for the work of the ministry. Twenty-six native lay teachers, Indian and Eskimo, were busily engaged in various parts of the diocese. Thousands of persons had been baptized into the membership of the Church, and showed by peaceable and upright lives that they were Christians in fact as well as in name.

LITERATURE.—*Hudson Bay*, by R. M. Ballantyne; *Forty-two Years amongst the Indians and Eskimo*, by Beatrice Batty (the Religious Tract Society); *John Horden: Missionary Bishop*, by the Rev. A. R. Buckland, M.A. (London: The Sunday School Union).

CHAPTER III

THE "PRAYING-MASTER" OF THE REDSKINS

"The Apostle of the North"—The backwoods schoolmaster—Indians and fur-traders—At Norway House—The "praying-master"—R. M. Ballantyne—A famous dog-train—Camping in the snow—The Arctic night—The talking birch bark—A tragic incident—An Indian mother's forgiveness—Adopted by the Chippeways.

WE have seen how, through the influence of Bishop Horden, Christianity was spread among the Indians and Eskimo around the inhospitable shores of Hudson Bay. But we have now to follow the story of a man whose journeys and adventures amidst the "snowflakes and sunbeams" of the Far North throw even those of Horden into the shade. Being a bishop, the latter naturally confined himself to his diocese; though a vast diocese it was. But James Evans, "the Apostle of the North," as he has been called, was not a bishop, and so was free to take for *his* diocese the length and breadth of half a continent. From Lower Canada to the Rocky Mountains, and from Lake Superior to the Arctic Circle, he pushed ever forward as a pioneer of Christianity to the Indian races of British North America. It is three-quarters of a century since he began those incessant labours which make him the modern successor of Brainerd

THE BACKWOODS SCHOOLMASTER

and Eliot. The wheatfields of Manitoba now wave where in those days vast herds of buffaloes roamed over the plains. The railway train and the steamboat have taken in some measure the place of the canoe and the dog-sledge. The fur-trader's lonely fort in the wilderness has been supplanted here and there by the flourishing, up-to-date Western city. And yet, after all, civilization has done little more than fringe the borders of those vast territories of the Canadian North-west through which James Evans journeyed unweariedly, whether in the long winter or the short summer, as he bore his message of peace and goodwill to the tribes of the Assiniboine and the Saskatchewan, to the fierce Blackfeet and Mountain Stonies of the Rockies, and even to those of the redskin peoples whose hunting-grounds lay under the North Star by the shores of Lake Athabasca or along the banks of the great Mackenzie River, which pours its mighty flood of waters into the Arctic Sea.

James Evans was an Englishman who, like many another, had gone to Canada in search of a career. Finding it difficult to get employment in business, he became a backwoods schoolmaster. It was a fine training for the life that lay before him, bringing not only experience as a teacher, but familiarity with those arts of the hardy backwoodsman which were by and by to stand him in good stead. He was a Wesleyan, and as the leaders of the Wesleyan Church in Canada came to know his talents and enterprise, as well as his Christian zeal, they offered him a post as teacher in one of their Indian schools in the Lake Ontario district. It was pioneer work of the purest kind, but Evans thoroughly enjoyed it, and

INDIANS AND FUR-TRADERS

lived happily in a tent with his young wife until he had felled cedar trees and sawn them into logs and built both school and schoolhouse with his own hands. His success as a missionary teacher led before long to his being ordained as a minister, and appointed to labour among the Indian tribes on the northern shores of Lake Superior. This involved a dangerous journey of many days in an open boat, but Evans was now an expert canoeist, who could handle a paddle as if to the manner born. He reached Lake Superior in safety, and began his lifelong fight against the superstitions and cruelties of Red Indian paganism at a place which bore the appropriate name of Devil's Hole.

To any ordinary man the far-stretching coasts of the greatest of all the American lakes would have been a field sufficient for a life's labours. But Evans was not an ordinary man. Like Livingstone in Africa, he was never satisfied unless he was continually pressing on into new regions, and carrying the name of Jesus Christ where it had not been heard before. And in the most unexpected way there came an opening and a call to a new and larger sphere such as he longed for.

The fur-traders of the great Hudson Bay Company, whose forts were scattered right across the continent from the Atlantic to the Pacific, and from the Great Lakes to the Arctic Ocean, had noticed for some time that many of the Indians of the north were drifting steadily southwards. This gave them much concern, for it was from the northern part of their territories that they got a large proportion of their most valuable furs, and this southerly movement of the native hunters threatened the Company

IN SEARCH OF A MISSIONARY

with serious loss. At first the migration was set down simply to a desire to escape to a more genial climate, but fuller investigation revealed that the true reason was very different. The Indians of the north had heard some word of a new and wonderful religion which had come to their brothers in the south—a religion given by the Great Spirit to the red man as well as to the white. Around many a camp-fire the tidings had been discussed. And at last religious curiosity became so strong that, in the words of Mr. Egerton Young, the biographer of Mr. Evans and one of his present-day successors, "family after family embarked in their birch canoes and started for the land of the South Wind, in order to find the teacher and the Book."

And so it occurred to the directors of the Company that it would be to their advantage to bring the missionary to the Indians, instead of leaving the Indians to go in search of the missionary. They applied accordingly to the Wesleyans in England to send without delay several suitable men to work among the tribes of the North-West. This the Wesleyan Society at once proceeded to do, and as the most competent man to be the leader of the movement their choice fell upon Mr. Evans. He lost no time in transferring himself from Lake Superior to Norway House, which is situated at the northern end of Lake Winnipeg, "The Lake of the Sea," and in those days was one of the Hudson Bay Company's most important forts.

As illustrating the conditions of life at that time in those remote regions of the British Empire, it is interesting to know how Norway House received its name. So great were the hardships and loneliness that had to be

AT NORWAY HOUSE

faced in the service of the Hudson Bay Company that few Englishmen cared for such employment. Hence, as a matter of fact, it was largely Scottish Highlanders and Islanders, or men from the fiords and fjelds of Norway, who manned the outlying forts. Norway House was originally occupied by a contingent of Norwegians, and it was in compliment to them that the title was given to the fort.

We cannot dwell on the long canoe journey of 1500 miles to the northern lake, though it included perils in the rapids, an adventure with a black bear, and dangers on Lake Winnipeg itself, which got its name from the Indians because of its great size, and the sudden storms which burst upon it and raise its waves to the height of ocean billows.

On reaching his destination, Mr. Evans was received with great kindness by the officials of the Company, and was soon plunged into the kind of work he delighted in. For here were Indians from far and near. Those of the district around the fort were called Swampy Crees, and were a splendid class of men both in physique and intelligence. But in addition to these there came to Norway House large bands of hunters from the warlike tribes of the Rocky Mountains, men who had come down the Saskatchewan in their canoes for more than 1200 miles. And here too were Indians of a more peaceful blood from the Mackenzie and Peace Rivers in the distant north. All came on the same errand. They brought for sale the skins and furs of bears and beavers, otters and ermines, black and silver foxes, and many other animals. And in exchange they carried back English goods which had

THE "PRAYING-MASTER"

come across the Atlantic and through the ice-packs of Hudson Straits and Hudson Bay, and, after being landed at York Factory, had been brought up country for many hundreds of miles with infinite toil by canoe and dog-train.

Evans turned his attention in the first place to the Indians of Lake Winnipeg itself. Their minds were full of superstitions. They believed in a *Kissa-Manetoo* or Good God, but also and still more strongly in a *Muche-Manetoo* or Evil Spirit, whose power was thought to be the greater of the two. They listened eagerly to the good news which the white preacher brought to their wigwams of a divine love which conquers all evil, and a Father in heaven to whom every one of His children, whether whiteskin or redskin, is equally dear.

It was more difficult, however, for the *Ayumeaookemow*, or "praying-master," as Evans was called, to get them not only to believe in the divine love, but to give up their own hatreds and cruelties and other wicked ways. There was one chief named Maskepetoon, a man of magnificent stature and strength, who liked Mr. Evans greatly, but said that this new religion was only fit for old women. "I will never be a Christian," he cried, "so long as there is a scalp to take or a horse to steal from the Blackfeet." He was a man of such an ungovernable temper that he scalped one of his own wives in a fit of displeasure. And yet this same man by and by met the murderer of his son on the prairie, and riding up to him, tomahawk in hand, said: "By all the laws of the Indian tribes you deserve to die; but I have learned that if we expect the Great Spirit to forgive us, we must forgive our enemies, and therefore I forgive you."

"By all the laws of the Indian tribes you deserve to die, but as I expect the Great Spirit to forgive me, I forgive you," said the chief Muskepetoon, who at an earlier date had sworn, "So long as there is a Blackfoot to scalp I will never become a Christian."

R. M. BALLANTYNE

But Evans not only taught the Indians religious truth, he taught them to work—a very necessary lesson. No doubt there were times when work seemed quite superfluous, for deer abounded in the forest and multitudes of buffaloes browsed on the prairie. There were seasons, however, when game was scarce, and times when the Indians perished by the score for lack of some other means of subsistence. Hitherto they had thought it a degradation for a hunter to engage in any kind of manual toil. But Evans introduced new ideals. He won their respect by his own skill as a shot, and then by his example induced them to till the fruitful soil and build themselves comfortable houses. By the shores of the Lake, and not far from Norway House, there sprang up the neat Indian village of Rossville, with its houses and gardens and school and church, which is still one of the largest and finest Indian missions in North America. Those who have read Mr. R. M. Ballantyne's *Hudson Bay* will remember his humorous and yet sympathetic account of an Indian school festival at Rossville, of which Mr. Evans was the presiding genius, and at which the famous writer of boys' story-books was himself present, when he was a young clerk in the service of the Hudson Bay Company.

And now Mr. Evans began to turn his attention to those far-off tribes which had their settlements along the foothills of the Rocky Mountains or the banks of the Mackenzie River. Now began those great expeditions by waterway or dog-trail which surpassed in extent even the historic journeys of the Apostle Paul, for Evans would undertake a circuit of five thousand or six thousand miles in a single season. It is these immense journeys through

A FAMOUS DOG-TRAIN

the unknown wilderness that provide the most romantic elements in the story of his life. It was by them that he became known among the Red Indians through all the regions of the North-West not only, like other Christian preachers, as the *Ayumeaookemow*, or "praying-master," but as the *Keche Ayumeaookemow*, the "great praying-master." At one time we find him in his canoe toiling upstream, or darting down the swift rapids with a thrill of dangerous delight to which the artificial joys of the modern water-chute cannot be compared for a moment. Again he is camping out on those rolling plains of the Far West which are now the most fruitful corn-fields in the world, but were then the special preserves of the buffalo. Sometimes, as he lay down at night, the roaring of the bulls in the immediate neighbourhood would be so loud and incessant that it was impossible to fall asleep. And often, as he closed his eyes, he knew that if the herd should be seized with a sudden panic and stampede in the direction of his little camp, nothing could save him and his companions from being trampled to death.

But it is his winter journeys by dog-train over the frozen snow that strike us most with a sense of adventure and romance. His favourite team of dogs was famous all over the land. They were hybrids—half dogs, half wolves, possessed of such strength that they could do their eighty or ninety miles a day, dragging a load of three hundred pounds or more. In harness they were easily controlled, and yet they were so fierce that they had always to be chained up at night; while through the summer, when sledging was over for the season, they were carefully shut up in a high stockade. Their savage disposition brought

Red Indians hunting Buffalo in Winter Time

CAMPING IN THE SNOW

about their death. One morning an old chief who had come to look for Mr. Evans opened the gate of the stockade-yard, thinking he might be inside. In a moment the wolf-dogs sprang upon him and mangled him to death before they could be beaten off. For this crime, of course, they were immediately shot.

Let us take one or two glimpses of a tour in the depths of winter. The sledge which glides so swiftly over the snow is shaped like a boy's toboggan, but is eight or ten feet long, about eighteen inches broad, and is drawn by a team of four powerful dogs. On a long journey two or three of these sledges are necessary, for a plentiful supply of provisions must be carried, as well as bedding and camp utensils.

As the train sweeps forward there is often not a landmark to be seen—nothing from horizon to horizon but a vast unbroken sheet of snow. But the Indian guide pushes on with confidence, led by an instinct which never fails him and is almost as mysterious as that by which the swallows flying south find their way across the trackless sea.

After a long day's drive through an air which is trying enough at 40, 50, or even 60 degrees below zero, though infinitely worse when accompanied by a wind sufficiently strong to raise the fine, powdery snow into a blinding, choking blizzard, both men and dogs are thankful when camping time comes with its prospect of rest and warmth and food. The camp is nothing more than a square hole in the deep snow, scooped out with snowshoes which have to serve a shovels. On three sides the snow is banked up, while or the forth a huge fire is kindled with logs cut from the

FROZEN VICTUALS

forest. The kettles are then filled with snow, and as soon as the snow is melted, a goodly junk of frozen buffalo or bear or beaver is popped into the largest kettle to be boiled. Meanwhile the dogs are being fed, mostly with frozen fish, which has first to be thawed before the fire; and if the night is unusually cold they are allowed to get on their dog-shoes, which are not unlike a boy's socks. For the privilege of getting on their shoes they often beg by howling piteously.

Supper is never luxurious, and is always taken under difficulties. When the cold is 50 degrees below zero, meat taken out of the boiling kettle freezes so fast that it has sometimes to be thrust back into the water two or three times in the course of a meal. The tea is flavoured with milk which is quite sweet, though it may be several months old, and is presented not in a milk-jug but in a bag, from which pieces of it are broken off with a hatchet as required. There is no lingering over the tea-cups, or rather the pans that do service in the wilderness for those symbols of civilization; and that for the very good reason that if the tea is not quickly drunk, it cannot be drunk at all, having already become solid.

After evening prayers and the evening song, there comes the process of going, or rather being put, to bed. An Indian has a knack of rolling himself up securely in a warm rug of rabbit skins, but a white man is the better for being tucked in. Mr. Evans's Indians always attended to this duty most carefully. They spread blankets and rugs over him, and tucked in his head as well as his shoulders and feet, leaving not the least chink for the entrance of the outer air at any point. Under such treatment Mr. Evans felt at first

SHOEING THE DOGS

Dog shoes are long mittens without the thumb. They are fastened to the leg by a piece of deerskin. They are put on when a dog hurts its foot on rough sharp ice or in any other way. The dogs like wearing them, especially in cold weather, when they will lie down on their backs and howl and whine to have them put on.

THE ARCTIC NIGHT

as if he were being suffocated, but he soon learned to adjust himself to the necessary conditions of safety. For there is a real danger to the sleeper in neglecting these precautions. Mr. Egerton Young tells of one restless traveller who could not lie still in his camp bed, and so shook his face free from the protecting blankets. Wakening by and by, he put his hand up and felt what he took to be the icy handle of an axe. It turned out to be his own frozen nose.

Sometimes in the night a snowstorm would come on, and the travellers would waken in the morning to find themselves completely buried; but to those properly wrapped up the dry snow did little harm. It was more discomposing when the wolves, as often happened, gathered in a grim circle round the camp fire and kept up their blood-curdling howl through all the hours of darkness. Then it was necessary that a watch should be kept, and that the watcher should rise every now and then and pile on a fresh supply of logs, for there is no better protection against a pack of wolves than the glow of a blazing fire.

On a long march Mr. Evans frequently slept during the day and travelled through the night. The reason for this was that the intense white glare of the snow, with the sunshine reflected from it, was apt to bring on a distressing complaint of the eyes called snow-blindness. At night there was no similar risk. Besides to a lover of nature there was a peculiar charm about the winter nights, especially in the sub-Arctic zone. Those northern nights were nearly always beautiful, whether the moon was flooding the world with a soft radiance, or the frosty stars sparkled like diamonds through an atmosphere of absolute

THE CREE SYLLABIC SYSTEM

purity, or the aurora flashed and blazed, sending its mysterious ribbons of coloured light pulsing up to the very zenith and filling even those who had seen it times without number with a sense of awe in the presence of a glory so unearthly.

But from these romantic wanderings of the "Apostle of the North" we must pass to notice another feature of his varied activities and another great item in the debt owed him by the Red Indians of British North America. He was not only an intrepid and indefatigable traveller, but a remarkable linguist and a man also of real inventive genius. A matter which troubled him greatly was the difficulty of teaching the Indians to read in the ordinary way. He brooded for years over the problem of inventing a simpler and easier path than that of the alphabet and the spelling-book, and at last hit upon the plan which is known as the Cree Syllabic System. Taking the Cree language as his model, he found that it contained only thirty-six principal sounds, and by devising thirty-six simple characters to represent these sounds, he made it possible for any Cree Indian who learned to identify the characters to read at once without further difficulty. No spelling was necessary, only the pronunciation of the sound that corresponded to the character.

The result was that in a very few days old and young alike were able to read. But next came the difficulty of supplying them with books. Evans had no materials for printing and no experience in work of this kind. But he begged from the traders at Norway House the thin sheets of lead with which their tea chests were lined. Then, having carved out models of his syllabic characters and

THE TALKING BIRCH BARK

made casts of them in clay, he melted the lead and poured it into the moulds; and so, after many failures, obtained a sufficient supply of type. Printing-ink he manufactured out of soot mixed with sturgeon oil. Paper he could neither get nor make, but he found that sheets of birch bark would serve his purpose very well. Finally, in lieu of a printing-press he begged the loan of a jack screw used for packing bales of furs, and with no better equipment than this, turned out the first books which his Indian flock had ever seen.

The excitement produced by these printed sheets of bark was immense, for it seemed to the people nothing less than magic that birch bark could "talk," and something still more wonderful that it could bring them a message from the Great Spirit Himself. The result was that thousands, young and old, became readers of God's Word. And when the Society in England realized the value of Mr. Evans's invention, he was furnished with a properly equipped printing-press, from which, year by year, there came a steady supply of Bibles and Testaments in the native tongue.

"The syllabic characters," says Mr. Egerton Young, "are still in use. The British and Foreign Bible Society now furnish all these Northern missions with Bibles and Testaments free of cost. Hundreds of Indians are reading out of them every day of the year. Missionaries to other tribes have utilized these syllabics for other languages by adding additional signs for sounds not found among the Crees. Methodists, Episcopalians, Moravians, Roman Catholics, and others use these syllabics of James Evans, and find them of incalculable value."

A TRAGIC INCIDENT

As illustrating both the remarkable character of the hero of this chapter and the kind of influence he exerted even over Indians who remained heathen, a tragic incident in his history is worthy of notice.

One day he was out in a canoe shooting ducks, along with a young Indian named Hassel, who had become a Christian. By some accident which he never understood his gun went off. The full charge entered the head of poor Hassel, who fell back dead into the canoe.

Mr. Evans's grief was terrible. The Indian was a Chippewayan, and all his people were heathen. As such they retained their superstitious beliefs and cruel customs, and held in particular that blood must be given for blood and life for life. But his sorrow and sense of responsibility for his companion's death made him feel that he must surrender himself to Hassel's relatives, even though, as he well knew, it might result in his being put to death himself. Accordingly he wound up all his personal affairs, made arrangements for the management of the Mission, and after a trying scene of farewell with his wife and daughter, set out all alone for the distant part of the country in which the Chippeways lived.

Reaching the encampment of the tribe, he asked for the wigwam of Hassel's father. When it was pointed out to him he entered, and sitting down on the ground told his sad story, tears of sorrow meanwhile trickling down his face. At once the tent was full of excitement. Grasping their tomahawks and drawing their knives, the men of the family cried out for the blood of this paleface who had slain their kinsman. But there was one person in the tent who had already resolved that the paleface

ADOPTED BY THE CHIPPEWAYS

should live. This was no other than Hassel's old mother herself. She had been stricken with anguish when she heard of her son's death, but she had watched the stranger's countenance, and listened to the tones of his voice as he told his story, and she knew by the instincts of love and of grief that Evans was the true friend of her boy, and that his sorrow for what had happened was not less sincere than her own. And so when the avengers of blood were about to spring upon him as he sat unresisting on the ground, she ran forward and, putting both her hands on his head, said firmly:—

"He shall not die. There was no evil in his heart. He loved my son. He shall live, and shall be my son in the place of the one who is not among the living."

And so the Christian missionary was actually adopted, after the Indian custom, into the tribe and family of these heathen Chippeways. For a time he remained in the wigwam with his new father and mother. And after he returned to his own family and work he still regarded himself as their son, given them in place of the son he had shot. He knew that Hassel, after becoming a Christian, had been very thoughtful of his parents, and had sent them a present from time to time. And though himself a poor man at the best, he made a point to the end of his life of sending regularly to his foster-parents what he regarded as their rightful share of his own yearly income.

LITERATURE.—*The Apostle of the North: Rev. James Evans*, by Egerton R. Young (London: Marshall Brothers); *Hudson Bay*, by R. M. Ballantyne (Thomas Nelson and Sons).

CHAPTER IV

IN THE LAND OF THE DAKOTAS

Hiawatha—Stephen and Mary Riggs—The Sioux Indians—Indian *teepees*—"Eagle Help"—The scalping-party—A sad experience—The return of the bison—The Indian rising—A dreadful flight—The Dakota prisoners—Preaching in the prisoners' camp—A transformation on the prairies.

THE title of the present chapter will remind those who have read Longfellow's *Hiawatha* of one of the most frequently recurring lines in that poem of melodious repetitions—repetitions which are intended to suggest the steady "rushing of great rivers," and the waterfall's monotonous music

> In the land of the Dacotahs,
> Where the Falls of Minnehaha
> Flash and gleam among the oak-trees,
> Laugh and leap into the valley.

But Longfellow's picture of the Dakotas and their country, though beautiful as poetry, is very misleading as to the realities of life among the uncivilized Indians of the Western States. He deliberately put their cruelty and squalor out of his mind, and set himself to weave their legends and traditions into a song of pure romance. The tale we have to tell in the following pages may

STEPHEN AND MARY RIGGS

justly claim to be a story of romance. It takes us to the land of Hiawatha and Minnehaha, the land of lakes and prairies and primeval forests, where "the curling smoke of wigwams" is seen rising through the trees. But it is in the first place a story of sheer reality. The merely imaginative side of the romance quite disappears, in the presence of Indian life as it was actually lived in the land of the Dakotas little more than half a century ago; and the true romance is seen to lie in the heroism and self-sacrifice of the young American missionary and his wife, who went out to the Far West in connexion with the American Board of Foreign Missions to spend their days in the midst of those fierce savages. Their life was one of constant toil, of frequent alarms, of hope long deferred. But they had the courage of faith, and also its quiet patience. And one of them at least was spared to see a transformation among the Dakotas which went beyond anything for which they had looked.

It was in the year 1837 that the Rev. Stephen Riggs and his wife Mary left their home in the Eastern States and started westwards to begin work among the Sioux, the leading branch of the great Dakota family of Red Indians. Their first destination was Fort Snelling, a lonely military outpost at the junction of the Minnesota River with the Mississippi, not far from the laughing Falls of Minnehaha, and on the very site of the future city of Minneapolis. It is strange to think that less than seventy years ago the spot which is now the centre of the commercial life of the North-Western States was then an outpost in the wilderness, more difficult of access than most places in Central Africa are to-day. The

INDIAN "TEEPEES"

greater part of the journey of 3000 miles they were able to make by water—first down the Ohio River and then up the Mississippi. But so slow was travelling at that time, especially on the Upper Mississippi, that it was not till three months after leaving Massachusetts that they reached Fort Snelling.

Not far from the Fort there was a Mission station, soon afterwards to be broken up by a furious and bloody war between the Sioux on the one side and the Ojjibeways and Chippeways on the other. Here the Riggses stayed for a few months to learn a little of the Dakotas and their language, and then set out with a waggon across the prairies towards a lake known as Lac-qui-parle, "The Speaking Lake," which lay some 200 miles farther to the west and near the border line between the present States of Minnesota and Dakota. For thirteen days they pushed steadily towards the setting sun, and at length reached the lake with the mysterious name, suggestive of the presence of some haunting spirit. There they joined another pioneer missionary, Dr. Williamson, and had a room assigned them in a log cabin which he had built in the midst of the *teepees* or wigwams of the Sioux nation.

Their first task was to seek the acquaintance of the inmates of those *teepees* which were scattered along the shores of Lac-qui-parle. Approaching a Dakota village of that time, one saw a number of conical tents made of buffalo skins, with smoke issuing from holes left at the top. Lifting the little door of skin, the only shelter of the inmates against a temperature which in winter often sank to twenty degrees below zero, the visitor found

"EAGLE HELP"

himself in a cold, smoky lodge about twelve feet in diameter, where, besides a dirty lounging warrior with his pipe, there might be "a mother and her child, a blanket or two, a skin, a kettle, and possibly a sack of corn."

The Indians did not give the white men any welcome. On the contrary, they regarded them as intruders into their country, from whom it was legitimate to steal everything they could lay their hands on. They resented, too, any attempts to interfere with their ancestral habits, and especially with their deadly feuds and murderous attacks upon the Indians of other tribes. There was a notable chief called "Eagle Help," a war prophet and war leader among the Dakotas, a man of unusual intelligence, and the very first of all the Sioux nation who learned from Mr. Riggs to read and write his own language. But when the lust of battle came upon him, as it periodically did, he was the most bloodthirsty of savages. Once when he was about to lead out a war-party against the Ojjibeways for the purpose of slaying and scalping the men and carrying off the women as captives, Mr. Riggs argued with him in vain, and finally said that if the Sioux went on the war-trail he would pray that they might not be successful. This so offended the chief that just before starting he and his men killed and ate two cows that belonged to the Mission. And when they returned from their expedition, after a long tramp during which they had not fallen in with a single Ojjibeway, he attributed this failure entirely to the white man's charms, and held himself justified accordingly in killing and eating another cow which still remained.

After spending five years at Lac-qui-parle in hard and

A SAD EXPERIENCE

unpromising labour, Mr. Riggs decided to push out still farther into the wilderness, and so removed to a district called Traverse des Sioux, where no missionary had ever been before. But if his experiences at Lac-qui-parle had been trying, those which he now had to encounter were tenfold worse. Accompanied by his wife's brother, a fine young man of twenty-two, by whom they had been joined, he went on in advance and pitched his tent among the Traverse Indians. Many of them objected to his coming, and even tried to drive him away by threats. But his mind was made up to stay, and with the help of his companion he began to cut and haul logs to build a little cabin. The Indians did not interfere with this; but as soon as the two men had felled their logs and painfully dragged them to the spot where they proposed to build, they came down in force demanding payment for the wood taken from the forest, and Mr. Riggs was obliged to give up some of his scanty stock of provisions.

Before the cabin was finished Mrs. Riggs and the children arrived, and their arrival was marked by an incident which left a deep and painful impression on the lady's mind. She was attended by three young Dakota Indians who had become Christians. Some distance from Traverse the road crossed the Chippewa River, and at this point, as one of the three Indians, whose Christian name was Simon, was riding on ahead of the little company, a war-party of Ojjibeways suddenly emerged from the forest, carrying two fresh and bleeding scalps. They came up to Simon and flourished their trophies in his face, but did him no harm, probably because they saw that he was in the company of white people, and vanished across the

A SAD EXPERIENCE

river as suddenly as they had appeared. Two miles farther on the road, Mrs. Riggs and her escort met a band of maddened Dakotas in wild pursuit of the Ojjibeways. They told Simon that one of the two scalps he had just seen was that of his own brother; and when they learned that the Ojjibeways were now beyond their reach, they turned their fury on Mrs. Riggs and her three Indian companions for not having tried to kill or stop the scalping-party. Brandishing their muskets in the air, they clustered with savage faces and angry cries round the waggon in which the lonely white woman sat with a child in her arms. Finally, they shot one of the two horses that composed the team, so that she had to get out and walk the rest of the way in the heat of the broiling sun, carrying her little girl in her arms. This was Mrs. Riggs' introduction to Traverse des Sioux, and it was only one of various similar episodes which helped to turn her dark hair prematurely grey.

A few days after, her brother was drowned while bathing in the swift river which flowed in front of the cabin. He was a youth of a joyful Christian spirit, and all that morning, while hard at work on the unfinished house, had been singing again and again a couplet from a simple but very appropriate hymn—

> Our cabin is small and coarse our fare,
> But love has spread our banquet here.

By and by he went down to the stream and plunged in for a swim before dinner, but took cramp, and was carried away by the current and drowned. And now in the midst of her weeping for the dead brother, Mrs. Riggs

RETURN TO LAC-QUI-PARLE

had to take his place in the task of finishing the log-house, working with her husband at the other end of the cross-cut saw, because there was no one else who could be got to do it.

It was a sad beginning to life in the new sphere, the forerunner, too, of many another hard experience, but the devoted pair never lost heart. The Dakotas killed their cows and horses, stole their goods, and sometimes threatened their lives. But they worked patiently on, doing their best to live down enmity and opposition. Gradually they made friends with one and another through the power of kindness, but found it difficult to get even the most friendly to become Christians. A redskin might acknowledge that Christianity was true, but the Christian commandments were too much for him. He could not give up his killing and stealing and polygamy. Or if he promised to live a Christian life and actually made a start upon the straight path, a visit to some white trader's settlement where whisky was to be had was enough to turn him into an incarnate devil once again, ready for the worst of his old evil ways, and using vile and insulting language even to the white lady who had done so much for his own women and children.

At length, after several years had been spent at Traverse, the departure of Dr. Williamson to another station made it necessary in the general interests of the Mission to the Dakotas that the Riggses should return to Lac-qui-parle. Their trials and hardships, however, did not cease with the change. The Indians robbed them as before, though sometimes, it must be confessed, the thieves had the excuse that they and their children were

A Red Indian pursuing a Bison

THE RETURN OF THE BISON

almost starving. Fortunately this excuse for stealing was taken away not long after their return. For several years the vast herds of bison, on which the Indians chiefly depended for their subsistence, had migrated farther and farther to the west, seeming to justify the complaint of the Dakotas that a curse fell upon their country with the coming of the white man's foot. But now the bison came back again, and all around Lac-qui-parle the hunters might be seen armed with bow and arrow and riding forth over the prairie to shoot down the noble game. For two years the Dakotas revelled in fresh buffalo meat, and were content to leave the white man's horse and cow alone. The children playing around the *teepees* grew sleek and fat. The very dogs got plump, and peace and contentment reigned on every hand.

But by and by the buffaloes began to move westwards again—a circumstance which the Dakotas might very well have attributed to their own deadly arrows rather than to the white man's foot. The redskin thieves resumed their work in the dark nights; and of all the forms of theft which they practised none was more trying than the spoliation of the gardens of the palefaces. It was hard to sow and plant, to weed and water, and after weeks of toil and months of watching to rise some morning and find that a clean sweep had been made of all the fruits and vegetables during the night. It almost seemed an allegory of what had been going on for years in the larger sphere of missionary labour. "We have sown our seed in toil and tears," Mr. Riggs and his wife said to each other, "but where is the fruit?" And yet it was

THE INDIAN RISING

just when the hope of much fruit was almost disappearing that fruit came most abundantly, though not in any anticipated way.

In the autumn of 1862 a body of 4000 Dakota Indians had gathered at an agency called Yellow Medicine to receive certain annuities from the Government to which they were entitled. But through some mismanagement at headquarters (not greatly to be wondered at, seeing that the tremendous struggle with the Southern States was absorbing all the energies of President Lincoln's administration at that very time) the annuity money had not come, and the agent could not say when it would arrive. He wished the Indians in the meantime to disperse again to their homes. But as their homes in many cases lay at a distance of a week's journey or more, they refused to go back, and they also demanded that while they were kept waiting they should be fed. By and by they grew unmanageable, and began to attack the stores and help themselves to provisions. Resistance being offered, they became violent, and several white men were killed. As soon as word of this outbreak reached the nearest fort, an officer of the United States Army hurried off with fifty men, hoping to quell the rising. But the Indians met this little company with alacrity, and easily defeated it. Half of the soldiers were killed, and the rest had difficulty in making good their escape. This victory over the regulars set the prairie on fire. All over the land of the Dakotas the red men rose against the whites.

Fortunately for the missionaries, the Indians who knew them best proved friendly towards them at this crisis, and did what they could to shelter them from the storm of

A DREADFUL FLIGHT

savagery which had burst over the country. The Riggses were smuggled stealthily to an island in the Minnesota River, where for a time they lay concealed. But their situation there was too precarious, and flight to the east was decided on. A terrible flight it was, especially for the women and children. The nearest place of safety was the town of Henderson, far down the Minnesota. They had to make their way cautiously, often in the dead of night, through the long grass of the trackless prairie, grass that was heavy and sodden with water, for it rained incessantly for nearly a week. Starvation stared the fugitives in the face again and again, but they found food more than once in cabins which had been hurriedly deserted by white settlers, and once, coming upon a cow left in a stable, they did not hesitate to kill it and cook themselves a hearty meal. All the time, by day and by night, there lay heavy upon their hearts the horror of the Red Indian pursuer with his tomahawk and scalping-knife. But they reached Henderson safely at last, where they were received by the inhabitants as persons alive from the dead. "Why, we thought you were all dead!" was the first greeting they received. And they found that a telegram had come from Philadelphia saying, "Get the bodies at any cost."

The Sioux rebels were defeated at last in a pitched battle, and 400 of them were taken prisoners. When brought before a military commission, 300 of these were found guilty of having deliberately taken up arms against the U.S. Government, and were sentenced to death. President Lincoln, however, who had the right of reviewing the findings of the commission, leaned towards

THE DAKOTA PRISONERS

clemency, and gave instructions that in the meantime only those should be executed who were proved to have taken part in individual murders or in outrages upon white women. These special crimes were brought home to thirty-eight of the prisoners, and an arrangement was made by which they were all hanged simultaneously in full view of the camp by the cutting of a single rope.

Through the crevices in the walls of their log prison-house the rest of the captives saw their comrades hanged. And the sight produced a profound impression upon them, an impression not only of fear, but in many cases of guilt. Mr. Riggs and Dr. Williamson, who had been present in the camp as interpreters from the first at the request of the commanding officer, found their time fully occupied in dealing with the prisoners, who listened to their message of the love of God and salvation through Christ for the sinful as no Indians had ever listened to them before. Formerly, even in church on the Lord's Day, the Dakotas had heard the most earnest preaching with an air of stolid indifference. They would never rise to their feet at any part of the service, and they continued smoking all the time. Now their whole demeanour was changed. And as the days passed, a wonderful wave of conversion passed through the camp, in which there were now gathered, in addition to the prisoners, some 1500 other Dakotas who were anxious about the fate of their friends. It was not long till 300 adult Indians in that camp made public profession of their faith in Christ, and were baptized into the communion of the Church. Eventually the prisoners were pardoned by the President and allowed to return to

A TRANSFORMATION

their homes. But the work begun by the missionaries under such strange circumstances at the close of the war still went on, and resulted in the Christianization of the greater part of the Dakotas.

A few years after the Sioux war was over brave Mary Riggs passed away, worn out by labours and sorrows. Her husband, however, was spared to see his name become an honoured one in America, and not only among the friends of Christian missions, but in academic circles as well. For this bold pioneer of the Church militant had also the instincts of an original scholar. Through all his years of frontier toil and peril, often with no better study than a room which served at the same time for kitchen, bedroom, and nursery, and no better desk than the lid of the meal-barrel, he had carried on laborious researches into the language of the Indians, which resulted at last in his *Dakota Grammar* and *Dakota Dictionary*, and brought him the well-deserved degrees of D.D. and LL.D. But his highest honours were written not in the records of Universities, but in the changed lives of the Dakota people. In his old age, looking back over forty years of service, he could trace a wonderful contrast between *then* and *now*. In 1837, when he came to the Far West, he was surrounded by the whole Sioux nation in a state of ignorance and barbarism. In 1877 the majority of the Sioux had become both civilized and Christianized. Then in the gloaming his young wife and he had seen the dusky forms of Indian warriors flitting past on their way to deeds of blood. Now the same race was represented not only by sincere believers, but by native pastors in the churches and native teachers in the schools. And on the

A TRANSFORMATION

same prairies where the war whoop of the savage had once been the most familiar sound, the voice of praise and prayer might be heard to rise with each returning Day of Rest from Indian cabins as well as Indian sanctuaries.

The story told in this chapter is drawn from Mr. Riggs' book, *Mary and I: Forty Years with the Sioux* (Chicago: W. G. Holmes).

CHAPTER V

IN THE FORESTS OF GUIANA

The Caribbean Islands—The Waraoons of the Orinoco—Kingsley's *At Last*—The tribes of Guiana—Rivers and *itabbos*—In the high woods—Swamps and forest bridges—Alligator and anaconda—The spotted jaguar—Humming-birds and fireflies, marabuntas and mosquitoes—The house in the palm tree—Legends and sorcerers—Cannibal mounds—A spiritual romance.

FOUR hundred years ago, when the beautiful West Indian Islands were first discovered by the white men, they were inhabited by various native races of which the most powerful were the Caribs, a fierce and cannibal people. The original home of the Caribs, according to all their own traditions, was on the mainland of South America, in the dense forests which stretch along the lower reaches of the great river Orinoco. From the wide mouths of that river they had issued from time to time in their war-canoes and swept like a storm cloud on the nearer islands of the West Indian Archipelago, killing and devouring the gentle and peaceful Arawaks and Waraoons who were in possession before them. In *Robinson Crusoe* we have the most vivid description in English literature of those cruel Caribs of long ago. For though Alexander Selkirk served as the prototype of Defoe's immortal story, and Juan Fernandez in the South Pacific was the island in

THE WARAOONS OF THE ORINOCO

which that Scottish buccaneer was marooned for several years, it is really one of the West Indian Islands, perhaps Tobago, that Defoe takes as the stage of Crusoe's exploits and experiences. The incident of the footprint on the sand, as well as the decidedly tropical vegetation of the island, is undoubtedly adopted from West Indian sources. And the cannibal scenes which are described with so much realism are probably derived from the writings of the early voyagers, who told of the inhuman habits of that savage Indian race which gave its name to the fair waters of the Caribbean Sea.

From the Caribbean Islands the old Indian races, both the conquering and the conquered, have now almost entirely disappeared. To find a pure-blooded representative of those primitive people whom Columbus and the other early discoverers found there at the close of the fifteenth century, we have to go to the forests of the South American mainland, to which the broken relics of the aboriginal West Indian peoples—Caribs, Arawaks, Waraoons, and the rest —were long since driven by the tyranny of the Spaniard. Within the recollection of the present writer, Waraoons of the Orinoco used still to come paddling once a year across the blue Gulf of Paria on a visit to the old home of their fathers in Trinidad—the nearest of all the West Indies to the South American Continent. He can remember, as a boy, going down with his father to the wharf at San Fernando to see these Waraoons arriving—statuesque, sadlooking savages, absolutely naked, who brought with them for barter articles of their own manufacture—hammocks of great strength such as they swung to the trees in their forest homes, baskets ornamented with stained porcupine

KINGSLEY'S "AT LAST"

quills skilfully woven into the framework, mats similarly embellished with "jumbie-beads"[1] and other wild seeds, red, black, or brown.

In his *At Last: A Christmas in the West Indies*, Kingsley gives a beautiful description of the annual visit of the Waraoons to Trinidad, although he had not the opportunity of seeing this curious sight for himself:—

"Once a year, till of late—I know not whether the sight may be seen still—a strange phantom used to appear at San Fernando. Canoes of Indians came mysteriously across the Gulf of Paria from the vast swamps of the Orinoco; and the naked folk landed and went up through the town, after the Naparima ladies (so runs the tale) had sent down to the shore garments for the women, which were worn only through the streets, and laid by again as soon as they entered the forest. Silent, modest, dejected, the gentle savages used to vanish into the woods by paths made by their kinsfolk centuries ago—paths which run, wherever possible, along the vantage-ground of the topmost chines and ridges of the hills. The smoke of their fires rose out of lonely glens as they collected the fruit of trees known only to themselves. In a few weeks their wild harvest was over, and they came back through San Fernando; made, almost in silence, their little purchases in the town, and paddled away across the Gulf towards the unknown wildernesses from whence they came."

In the forests of Guiana the Society for the Propagation

---

[1] Why "jumbie-beads" are so called by the Trinidad children who play with them the writer is unable to say. A "jumbie" is a spirit or ghost. Thus on every negro's grave a plant called the "jumbie-bush" used to be planted, presumably to keep ghosts from rising.

THE TRIBES OF GUIANA

of the Gospel has long carried on a most interesting work among the Caribs, Arawaks, Waraoons, and other Indian tribes which still represent those island aborigines around whom gathers so much of the romance and tragedy of early West Indian history. None of the Society's agents has been more diligent or successful than the Rev. Mr. Brett, whose *Mission Work in Guiana* is a standard book on the subject of the Indian races of Venezuela and British Guiana. We shall follow Mr. Brett as he tells us something of his canoe voyages on the rivers and *itabbos* of the Essequibo district, of his tramps through the tropical forests and swamps, of dangers from pumas and jaguars by land and alligators and *camudis* by water, of the ways and thoughts of the Indian folk, and the power of religious truth to deliver them from the tyranny of immemorial superstitions and make them good Christians as well as law-abiding British subjects.

It is more than sixty years since Mr. Brett began his labours among the Indians of Guiana, and his task was beset in those early days by many serious difficulties. One was the wild character of the people, and their hostility, the hostility especially of their sorcerers, to the teachers of a new religion. Mr. Youd, a predecessor of Mr. Brett's, had received a gift of poisoned food from one of those sorcerers, with the result that he and his whole family were poisoned. His wife and children all died, and though he himself lingered on for a few years, it was in shattered health; while he too eventually succumbed to the fatal influences in his blood.

Another difficulty was caused by language, for in penetrating into the country the traveller, as he leaves the

RIVERS AND "ITABBOS"

coast and plunges into the forest, passes rapidly from one tribe to another, all speaking different tongues. Nearest to the sea are the Waraoons and the Arawaks, farther inland are the Caribs, beyond these are the migratory Acawoios, who do not live in villages, but wander through the woods with their deadly blow-pipes, by means of which they bring down from the highest trees the birds, monkeys, and other animals that they use for food. Mr. Brett found it necessary to learn four Indian languages, none of which had ever before been reduced to a written form. And not only did he master them for himself, but prepared grammars and vocabularies which made the task of his successors infinitely easier, and also translated into all of them large parts of the New Testament.

Not the least of the difficulties was that of travelling in such a country. It involved laborious and often dangerous canoe voyages, and weary tramps through dense forests which at certain seasons were converted into dismal swamps. But Mr. Brett had the true enthusiasm and pluck of the pioneer missionary, and seems to have considered the hardships that fell to his lot as all " in the day's work."

Guiana is a land of many rivers, and this makes canoeing the chief method of travelling, especially as the forests themselves become inundated after the rains, and it is then possible to cross from river to river by means of passages called *itabbos*. In this way, for example, an Indian crew can paddle across country from the Essequibo to the mouth of the Orinoco, a distance of two or three hundred miles.

It is not all plain sailing, however, in a voyage of this kind. Every few minutes the Indians have to use their cutlasses to lop away the network of interlacing branches

DANGERS OF THE FORESTS

and creepers which the prodigal growth of the tropics weaves so quickly from side to side of the narrow waterway. Sometimes again the passage is blocked by a great fallen tree, and then the missionary must lie down in the bottom of the canoe while his boatmen try to thrust it underneath the barrier. This has to be done as quietly and swiftly as possible, for fear of disturbing any venomous snake which may have taken up its abode in a hollow of the decaying trunk.

But canoeing was not always feasible, and then would begin the tramp through the forests—those mysterious and awesome "high woods of the tropics" of which Kingsley writes with such enthusiasm. To the inexperienced traveller in this wilderness of rank vegetation majestically confused there sometimes comes the fear of being lost, for he feels his own helplessness as to direction, and knows that but for the instinct of his Indian guides he would soon go utterly astray. He is bewildered, too, by the multiplicity of strange sounds. Parrots are screeching, monkeys are chattering, *cigales* are piping on a high note which suggests a shrill steam-whistle, insects innumerable are chirping and whirring; while at times, perhaps, there comes a noise like a muffled crash of thunder, which tells that some ancient giant of the woods has fallen at last.

The forests of Guiana are full of swamps, and when Mr. Brett came to these there was nothing for it but to take off his shoes and socks, sling them round his neck, and wade on through mud and slime. Repeated soakings often made his feet swell so badly that it was hardly possible to pinch them into shoes again, and he found it

SWAMPS AND FOREST BRIDGES

easier simply to go barefooted like an Indian. But this also had its disadvantages, for alternate wading through marshes and walking with bare feet over the burning sandy soil brought on painful blains which, unless great care was taken, would pass into ulcers. Sometimes the swamps were so deep that they could not be waded, and the only means of crossing was by trees cut down and thrown across. These primitive forest bridges, which are also used for crossing the smaller streams and ravines, are often of considerable length. Mr. Brett tells of one which he measured, the trunk of a mora tree, which was 108 feet long from the place where the trunk was cut to the point at which the lowest branches began to spring. The Indians are quite expert at walking on these slippery pathways, but to a European with his boots on they present a formidable task. Mr. Brett's Indian companions were sometimes quite anxious about him, and on one occasion exhorted him to "hold on with his feet," forgetting that toes encased, as his were, in a good thick sole are of no use for prehensile purposes.

Apart from the malarial fevers to which in those low-lying tropical regions a European is constantly liable, the chief dangers encountered by Mr. Brett in his journeys into the interior came from the wild animals which swarm in Guiana, both on land and water There are alligators of various sorts which, as amphibious creatures, are dangerous on both elements. Mr. Brett tells of one which made its nest in his own churchyard, and rushed savagely one evening at an assembly of mourners gathered round a grave, just after he had finished reading the burial service, scattering them in all directions. But not

THE SPOTTED JAGUAR

less dreaded than the alligator is the great anaconda, or *camudi*, as the Indians call it, a species of water-boa which swims like an eel, and grows to the length of thirty feet. In the water the *camudi* is more than a match for the alligator itself, and has been known even to attack persons who were inside a canoe. One Sunday morning an exciting fight took place in mid-stream between a *camudi* and an alligator, exactly in front of a chapel on the bank of the river Pomeroon in which Mr. Brett was conducting divine service. At the news of the fight his congregation deserted him to a man, and even he could not resist the temptation to follow them as speedily as possible to the scene of action. The battle went on desperately for a long time, but at last the *camudi* succeeded in getting that deadly grip with its tail which gives it full purchase for its gigantic strength, and then it drew its coils tighter and tighter round the body of its formidable antagonist until the life of the alligator seemed to be completely squeezed out. At this point one of the onlookers, who had a gun and was a good marksman, fired and killed the *camudi*, which sank to the bottom. The alligator drifted ashore by and by, with its ribs crushed in, and in a dying condition, when it too was dispatched.

Besides the labaria, a very deadly snake which lurks among bushes or in the holes of old trees, the traveller through the forests has always to be on his guard against the puma and the jaguar. The puma is a formidable beast, but the great spotted jaguar is the tiger of South America, and is not much inferior in size or ferocity to the tiger of the Indian jungle. It is very destructive of goats, sheep, and cattle; and Mr. Brett tells us that he

A TITANIC COMBAT

Hearing a noise outside during service, Mr. Brett's congregation without ceremony went out to find a battle between an alligator and an enormous anaconda in progress. They had a long and terrific struggle, but at last the anaconda got into a position which enabled it to use its powers of compression to the utmost, and it literally crushed the life out of its opponent, only to be shot itself by a native.

MARABUNTAS AND MOSQUITOES

has often seen its footmarks in the morning on the moist ground all round a house—showing how it had been prowling about through the night in search of prey. The jaguar does not hesitate on occasions to attack men, and within Mr. Brett's own knowledge several persons lost their lives in this way, being both killed and devoured. Its habit of concealing itself in a tree and making its deadly spring from that coign of vantage upon any animal that passes underneath renders great caution necessary in going along the forest ways. It has a wholesome dread of the rifle, however, and the march of civilization is driving it farther and farther into the recesses of the woods.

But there are smaller creatures of the tropics for which civilization and the rifle have no terrors. There are myriads of butterflies, of course, which flutter past on wings of crimson and gold; darting humming-birds, with ruby or emerald breasts gleaming in the sunlight; fireflies which come out at dusk, and flit to and fro with their soft twinkling lights in the warm night air that is heavy with the breath of flowers. If the tiny creatures of the tropic woods were all like these, the traveller might fancy himself in a kind of Earthly Paradise. But what of the marabuntas—which Trinidad boys used to call "marrow-bones," from some idea that the stings of these fierce wasps, which are fond of building their clay nests in the corners of the white man's verandah, would penetrate to that region of the juvenile anatomy? What of scorpions, centipedes, tarantulas, blood-sucking bats, *bêtes rouges*, chigoes or "jiggers," and biting ants, whether black, white, or red? Worst of all, what of the ubiquitous,

THE HOUSE IN THE PALM TREE

irrepressible, unconquerable mosquito, which sometimes almost drives its victims mad, and whose victories over man, its mortal foe, deserve to be sung in the notes of its own musical humming and written with the blood of its helpless victims in some epic of the jungle? Mr. Brett does not exaggerate in the least when he reckons insect and other small annoyances among the most serious trials of missionary life in the inland districts of British Guiana. What sensitive white-skinned people have suffered from mosquitoes alone may be judged from this. At the season when the mosquitoes were at their worst, Mr. Brett's Indian crew, after a long and hard day's pull up the river, would sometimes paddle through the night for many a weary mile to the river's mouth and out to the open sea, in the hope of escaping for two or three hours from the stings of these excruciating pests.

Of the Indian tribes described by Mr. Brett, the Waraoons are in some respects the most interesting, precisely because they are the most primitive. When Sir Walter Raleigh was passing through the channels of the Orinoco delta in search of his imaginary El Dorado, he and his men were astonished to see fires burning high up in the air under the leafy crowns of palm trees. These were the hearth fires of the Orinoco Waraoons, who become tree-dwellers for several months of the year when their country is turned into a vast sheet of muddy water. Building a platform far up the stem of a palm tree, under the shelter of its overarching fronds, they plaster a part of this platform with clay to serve as a hearth, and sit smoking contentedly in their airy habitations, except at such times as they feel disposed to slip down into a canoe

MAKING POISONED ARROWS IN THE GUIANAS

LEGEND OF THE WARAOONS

so as to visit a friend in a neighbouring tree or go out fishing with a view to supper.

The Waraoons of Guiana are not tree-dwellers, for the floods on their rivers are not so severe as to make this necessary. But they are just as simple and unsophisticated as their brethren of the Orinoco. Except when Europeans come into their neighbourhood and set up a standard and a rule of social decency, both men and women go absolutely naked. They are gentle and unwarlike, even as their forefathers were three or four centuries ago when the Caribs swept down upon them and drove them into the swamps. While skilful in their own arts of canoe hollowing and hammock weaving, they are extremely easy-going in their way of life, and combine a good-natured disposition with a vein of humour which is somewhat rare among the Indian peoples. Like all other Indians, they have a genuine belief in the Great Spirit, and they have many legends of their own about Him and His dealings with men. The account they give of their origin is striking —though with a touch of the grotesque humour which characterizes them. The Waraoons, they say, originally dwelt in a country above the sky. The arrow of a bold hunter, falling by chance through a hole, revealed to this hunter the existence of the lower world. Making a rope of cotton, he descended by it to the earth, and when he climbed up again brought such a glowing report of the game that swarmed in earthly forests that the whole race was tempted to come sliding down the cotton rope out of the Paradise above. The last to make the attempt was a woman, and she, being fat, stuck in the hole and could neither squeeze herself through nor yet struggle back

OPPOSITION OF SORCERERS

again. There she remains to this day; and that is the reason why the human race cannot even peep through the hole in the sky into the world above. A curious version, we may think, of the story of Paradise Lost, and an equally curious version of woman's responsibility for the absolute closing of the gates of Eden.

Among all the Indian tribes of Guiana *piai* men, or sorcerers, are the priests of religion. The *piai* man corresponds to the "medicine man" of the North American Indians and the "obeah man" of Africa. No one dares to oppose him in anything, for he is an expert in poisons, and his enemies have a way of dying suddenly. In sickness, the most implicit confidence is placed in his powers, which to some extent are medicinal no doubt, for he generally has a real acquaintance with the healing virtues of the plants of the forest, but to a much greater degree are supposed to be supernatural. His special function is to drive away the evil spirit that has taken possession of the sick man. This he does by rattling a hollow calabash containing some fragments of rock crystal—an instrument of magical efficacy and the peculiar symbol of the *piai* man's office, by chanting a round of monotonous incantations, and by fumigating the patient plentifully with tobacco smoke, the incense of this "Indian weed" being firmly believed to exert a potent if mysterious influence.

It was naturally from these *piai* men that the strongest resistance came to the introduction of Christianity among the Indians of Guiana. One of them, as has been mentioned already, poisoned an English missionary and his family; and Mr. Brett himself was frequently warned that the sorcerers were going to *piai* him also. Instead of this

—87—

CANNIBAL MOUNDS

a strange thing happened. Saccibarra ("Beautiful Hair"), the chief of the Arawaks and their leading sorcerer, became disgusted with the tricks and hypocrisies of his profession, broke his *marakka* or magical calabash rattle, and came to Mr. Brett's hut, asking to be taught about "the Great Our Father, Who dwelleth in heaven." By and by he was baptized, receiving, instead of his heathen name, the Christian name of Cornelius. Cornelius the Arawak was a man of great intelligence, and it was with the aid of this converted Indian and his family that Mr. Brett was able to carry through his first efforts at translation. Still better things ensued, for five other sorcerers followed the example of Cornelius, gave up their *marakkas* to Mr. Brett in token that they had renounced the practice of magic, and became faithful and useful members of the Christian Church. Evangelists arose among the Indians themselves. Chapels sprang up here and there in the depths of the forest—two of them, as was accidentally discovered at a later stage, having been built on ancient cannibal mounds. Struck by the appearance of these mounds, Mr. Brett was led to undertake a little excavation; and his researches speedily proved that the very spots where the House of God now stood and Christ's Gospel was preached from Sunday to Sunday had once been the kitchen middens of large cannibal villages. There, heaped together, were the skulls and other bones of human beings slaughtered long ago, these skulls and bones being invariably cracked and split in a way which showed that the hungry cannibals in their horrible feasts had eaten the very brains and marrow of their victims.

We speak of the romance of missions; and even from

A SPIRITUAL ROMANCE

the most external point of view they are often full of the romance that belongs to all heroism and adventure. But to those who look deeper the spiritual romance is the most wonderful—the transformation of character and life, the turning of a savage into a Christian. In the Pomeroon district of Guiana, the centre of Mr. Brett's labours, more than five thousand persons have been brought into the Church through baptism. As for the moral and spiritual effect of his patient and heroic exertions, we may cite the testimony of the Pomeroon civil magistrate, who at first did not encourage Christian work among the Indians:—

"A more disorderly people than the Arawaks," he wrote, "could not be found in any part of Guiana. Murders and violent cases of assault were of frequent occurrence. Now the case is reversed. No outrages of any description ever happen. They attend regularly divine service, their children are educated, they themselves dress neatly, are lawfully married, and as a body there are no people in point of general good conduct to surpass them. This change, which has caused peace and contentment to prevail, was brought about solely by missionary labour."

The chief authority for this chapter is Mr. Brett's *Mission Work in Guiana* (London, S.P.C.K.). Reference has also been made, however, for some points to *Ten Years of Mission Life in British Guiana*, by the Rev. W. T. Veness (S.P.C.K.), and *Protestant Missions in South America*, by Canon F. P. L. Josa and others (New York, Student Volunteer Movement).

CHAPTER VI

THE SAILOR MISSIONARY OF TIERRA DEL FUEGO

"The Neglected Continent"—The despised Fuegian—Darwin's testimony — Captain Allen Gardiner — South American Missionary Society—A sly Patagonian—An exploring expedition—The final enterprise—At Banner Cove—How the tragedy came about—The *cache* in the rocks—Spaniard Harbour—The end—Search and discovery—The diary—Victory through death.

IF from the point of view of Christian evangelization South America has justly been called " The Neglected Continent," there is no part of it to which until modern times the description more fitly applied than that southern portion of the mainland called Patagonia, together with the large archipelago of closely huddled islands which projects still farther towards the Antarctic Ocean, and is known by the rather inappropriate name of Tierra del Fuego, or " Land of Fire."[1]

The inaccessibility and desolation of the whole region, and the ferocious and almost inhuman character of the tribes encountered by vessels passing through the Straits of Magellan, which divide Fuegia from the mainland, for

[1] The name was given to the group by Magellan, who discovered the islands in 1520. It is supposed to have been suggested to him either by volcanic flames which are now extinct, or by the numerous fires kindled by natives which he saw along the coasts.

DARWIN'S TESTIMONY

long made any thoughts of carrying the Christian Gospel to this part of the heathen world seem absolutely visionary. The Fuegians in particular were looked upon as degraded almost beyond the hope of recovery. Travellers dwelt on their stunted figures, their repulsive faces, their low grade of intelligence, their apparent lack of natural affection, as shown by the readiness of parents to throw their children overboard in a storm in order to lighten a canoe, or of children to eat their own parents when they had grown old and useless. Darwin, the most careful of observers, spent some time in the Magellan Straits in the course of his famous voyage in the *Beagle*, and he records the conviction that "in this extreme part of South America man exists in a lower state of improvement than in any other part of the world." "Viewing such men," he says on another page of his *Journal*, "one can hardly make oneself believe that they are fellow-creatures and inhabitants of the same world." Of their speech he writes: "The language of these people, according to our notions, scarcely deserves to be called articulate. Captain Cook has compared it to a man clearing his throat, but certainly no European ever cleared his throat with so many hoarse, guttural, and clicking sounds."

And yet, through the enterprise begun and inspired by that heroic man of whom we have now to tell, the almost unpronounceable sounds of the Fuegian speech have been reduced to writing and made to convey the story of the Gospels, while the Fuegians themselves have been changed from murderous cannibals and thieves into peaceful, honest, and industrious members of a Christian community. When Darwin learned, on the unimpeachable

CAPTAIN ALLEN GARDINER

authority of a British admiral, of the extraordinary difference which a few years had made in the habits of these people, whom he had once been inclined to regard as possibly furnishing a missing link between the monkey and the man, he confessed his astonishment. "I could not have believed," he wrote, "that all the missionaries in the world could ever have made the Fuegians honest," and he went on to speak of this transformation as one of the wonders of history. More than this. Though not by any means a professing Christian, nor an advocate in general of Christian missions, he became from that time a regular subscriber to the funds of the society with whose founder we are at present concerned—" about as emphatic an answer to the detractors of missions," the *Spectator* once remarked, "as can well be imagined."

Allen Gardiner was an ex-captain of the British Navy. As a midshipman he had distinguished himself during a fierce engagement in 1814 between his ship, the *Phœbe*, and an American man-of-war, in which the British vessel was victorious; and he had risen step by step to the position of commander. When about forty years of age, however, he determined to abandon his chosen profession and devote the rest of his life to work among the heathen, by whose wretched condition he had been deeply impressed as a Christian man in the course of his many voyages in all parts of the world.

He turned first of all to South Africa, and had some interesting experiences among the subjects of Dingaan, the redoubtable Zulu chief. But war broke out between the Zulus and the Boers, and he was forced to leave the country. Several years thereafter were spent in the search for a suitable field of operations among the most neglected peoples of the world. We find him for a time on the coast of New Guinea, where, if he had not been thwarted by the Dutch officials, who had not the slightest sympathy with his aims, and declared that he might as well try to instruct monkeys as the natives of Papua, he might have largely anticipated the splendid work which was afterwards accomplished by the heroic "Tamate."

But it was in the Western, not in the Eastern, Hemisphere that the great work of his life was to lie, and it was towards South America in particular that his steps were now guided. He was not drawn, however, in the first instance towards the Straits of Magellan, but to the brave Araucanian tribes of the Pampas and the Cordilleras. Two or three years were spent in toilsome and dangerous journeys through bristling forests and swampy jungles, and over well-nigh impassable mountains, where precipices yawned on one hand, while on the other avalanches of snow or rock threatened to hurl the traveller to destruction. But though he met with many kindnesses from the natives, he found wherever he went that the Romish friars and priests poisoned the minds of the ignorant people against him and prevented him from being allowed to settle down among them. And so he had to go forth again in search of his proper sphere.

It was at this stage that he began to think of that dreary and desolate region in the neighbourhood of Cape Horn, which as a sailor he had more than once visited, and with which in the history of modern missions his name will for ever be associated. How to get there was his first difficulty, and it was a difficulty which only an

RETURN TO ENGLAND

experienced and skilful seaman could have overcome. He chartered a crazy old schooner, the owners of which regarded her as no longer fit to go to sea, and though still further hampered by a drunken and troublesome crew, succeeded in reaching the Straits of Magellan in March, 1842. He had provided himself with a few stores, and his plan was to settle on one or other of the islands and try to win the confidence of the inhabitants. How difficult this task would be he soon discovered. Wherever he landed, whether on the islands or on the Patagonian coast, the Indians showed themselves so unfriendly that he realized the impossibility of making any headway without some help and some more adequate equipment. He resolved accordingly to return to England without delay, and try to persuade one or other of the great missionary societies to take Patagonia and Tierra del Fuego under its care.

Unfortunately not one of the existing societies was in a position at that time to undertake any fresh responsibilities. But Gardiner, nothing daunted, next made his appeal to the Christian public, and succeeded at last in originating on a very humble scale what is now known as the South American Missionary Society. He undertook to labour, as he had always done before, at his own expense, but the Society furnished him with an assistant in the shape of a catechist named Mr. Hunt.

Embarking in a brig called the *Rosalie*, which was to pass through the Magellan Straits, these two devoted men were landed with their stores about three months after on the south coast of Patagonia, and there left to their own devices. For a time they could see nothing of any

AN UNFRIENDLY CHIEF

natives, though they lighted fires in the hope of attracting notice. Meanwhile they set to work to build huts in which to shelter themselves; and shortly after they had completed this task received some troublesome visitors in the persons of a chief whose name was Wissale, his wives and children, and a party of followers. Wissale, who had picked up a few words of English from passing ships, combined unbounded greed with a good deal of slyness. He soon began to make matters exceedingly uncomfortable for the two Englishmen. His intention apparently was to force his company upon them, especially at meal times, and compel them to put their scanty stores at his disposal. He came into the hut attended by his patriarchal family, and placing one child in Captain Gardiner's arms said, "This your son Hontechi"; while he handed another to Mr. Hunt with the remark, "Mitter Hunt, this your son Lux." From greed and impudence he gradually passed to threats of violence, and it was speedily evident to the two unfortunate philanthropists, not only that their provisions would soon be eaten up, but that in the mood of Wissale and his men their lives were hanging by a very slender thread. In this state of matters a passing ship bound for Valparaiso seemed to be providentially sent. Captain Gardiner felt that he had no alternative but to confess himself defeated, and once more to return to England.

The members of the Patagonian Society, as the South American Society was originally called, were much discouraged. The leader of their forlorn hope, however, never for a moment lost heart. "Hope deferred, not lost," is now the Society's motto: and the faith embodied

TYPES OF PATAGONIAN WOMEN

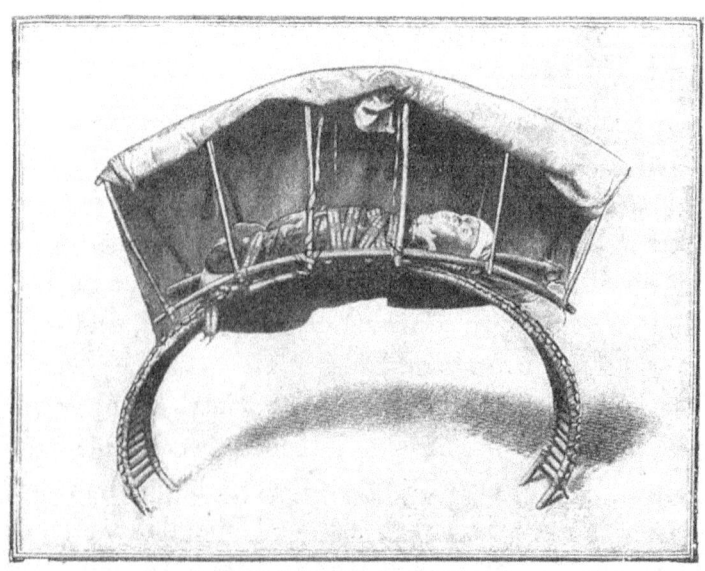

A NATIVE CRADLE IN PATAGONIA

AN EXPLORING EXPEDITION

in these words was the faith by which Gardiner lived. In the meantime he volunteered to see whether anything could be done among the Indians of Bolivia, and flung himself into this new departure with characteristic energy, until one of those domestic revolutions which are so common in the history of South American republics drove him out of the country, and made him feel once again that Tierra del Fuego was his Macedonia which was calling to him for help.

On this occasion, having raised the necessary funds by his own exertions, he persuaded the Society to allow him to take out a party of four sailors and a ship's carpenter. He intended the expedition to be in a measure one of exploration, the special purpose being to see whether a suitable base of operations could not be secured, and what would be the best method of reaching the scattered tribes of the archipelago. Owing to his former connexion with the Navy he had some influence at headquarters, and by this means one of Her Majesty's ships, the *Clymene*, which was about to sail for Peru, was placed at his disposal.

The *Clymene* reached Magellan Straits at a time when a hurricane of wind was blowing, accompanied by violent storms of sleet and hail; but after suffering severely from exposure to the inclement weather, Captain Gardiner was able to select a spot for his proposed station in a cove to which he gave the name of " Banner Cove " (with reference to Psalm LX. 4). The friendly warship, however, had not yet proceeded on her voyage when a band of natives came down on the little party encamped on the shore in so hostile and threatening an attitude that Gardiner felt

VISITS GERMANY AND SCOTLAND

that he must decide immediately whether it would be right to remain in this situation without any possible means of escape in the event of an attack. He had only a few hours in which to make up his mind, and the conclusion he came to was that he had no right to run the risk of sacrificing the lives of his five companions. He now began to realize that the only way in which he could hope to evangelize Fuegia was by having a vessel of his own, on board of which he might live when necessary, and be free at the same time to move about among the islands. Accordingly, he re-embarked with his party on the *Clymene*, and continued his voyage to Peru, from which he made his way homeward *via* Panama and the West Indies.

Though his new idea filled him with fresh enthusiasm, his enthusiasm was not widely shared. At this we can hardly wonder. There are not many persons who possess a hero's indomitable courage together with the perseverance of Bruce's spider. Some of the Captain's best friends advised him to give the whole thing up. "Only with my life," was his reply. Finding so little prospect of help in England, he went over to Germany and tried to enlist the sympathies of the Moravian Brethren; but though deeply impressed by the man and his story, and very anxious to do what they could, they were obliged to abandon the thought of giving him any practical aid. He next visited Scotland, and laid his plans before the mission boards of the three great Presbyterian Churches, but none of them felt free to plunge into a new and difficult undertaking. At this juncture, just when the prospects were most unpromising, a lady in Cheltenham came forward with a

THE FINAL ENTERPRISE

munificent donation, while at the same time several exceedingly suitable offers of personal service were received by the Society. The result was that a party of seven was made up which included, besides Captain Gardiner himself, Mr. Williams, a surgeon; Mr. Maidment, a Sunday-school teacher; three Cornish fishermen, and the ship's carpenter who had taken part in the previous expedition. Further, in accordance with the leader's plans, two strong double-decked launches were provided, either of which could furnish sleeping accommodation for the whole party.

Having taken passage from Liverpool in the *Ocean Queen*, Captain Gardiner and his companions with their stores and boats were landed in Banner Cove on December 17th, 1850. Writing by the *Ocean Queen*, which left next day for California, Gardiner says, in the last letter which his friends in England were ever to receive: "Nothing can exceed the cheerful endurance and unanimity of the whole party. I feel that the Lord is with us, and cannot doubt that He will own and bless the work which He has permitted us to begin."

From that point all communication with the outer world absolutely ceased. From the hour when they stood in their two launches, the *Pioneer* and the *Speedwell*, waving their last farewells to the departing ship, those seven brave men were never seen by friendly eyes in life again. It was in the awful loneliness and desolation of those barren islands and bleak southern seas that the tragedy was enacted of which we have now to tell.

When the party landed they were provided with necessaries for only half a year, the arrangement being that

AT BANNER COVE

early in 1851 supplies for the other six months should be dispatched from England. Early in January the Society began to make inquiries about a vessel, but to their dismay not one could be got to undertake the commission. From every quarter to which they applied the answer came, "No vessel would risk her insurance by attempting to land so small a freight as your stores in such a place as Tierra del Fuego." Matters were now growing very serious, for ocean telegraphs were still things of the future, and those were the slow days of sailing ships. Application was made to the Admiralty in the hope of getting the goods conveyed by one of their vessels. At the time, however, no Government ship was commissioned to that quarter of the world, and it was not till the last day of October, 1851, more than a year after the departure of the *Ocean Queen* from Liverpool, that H.M.S. *Dido* left Devonport with the belated stores on board. By that time Captain Gardiner and every member of his party had already been starved to death, and their unburied corpses were lying here and there along a wild and rocky shore.

But we must now return to Banner Cove and follow the story as it lies revealed in Gardiner's own diary. Having landed with some difficulty owing to a sudden gale which sprang up before the *Ocean Queen* was out of sight, the seven pioneers succeeded in making a *cache* among the rocks without being observed by the natives. Here they deposited a reserve stock of provisions, thinking it safer to do this than to keep everything stored in the launches. Not long after the Fuegians made their appearance. Several war-canoes gathered in the bay, the men on board

SPANIARD HARBOUR

being all armed with spears, and it was clear from their demeanour that nothing but their dread of guns kept them from attacking instantly, and that they were only waiting for a suitable opportunity to make a sudden and overwhelming rush. The Captain accordingly resolved, though with great reluctance, to leave Banner Cove, and sailed to another inlet known as Spaniard Harbour. A few days after their arrival in that place, one of those violent hurricanes sprang up for which the region all around Cape Horn is so notorious. The boats were torn from their anchorage and dashed ashore. The stores and bedding were much damaged, but were secured and transferred to a damp cave. Here the whole party slept for two nights, with the result that every one of them was attacked by severe rheumatism. Meanwhile, the *Pioneer* had been driven high up on the beach in so disabled a condition as to be past repairing, and it was decided to let her lie where she was and use her cabin as a sleeping-place.

Troubles now began to thicken. Scurvy broke out—a deadly disease for men in such a situation, and not long after provisions began to run short. Now and then a few fish were caught, or an occasional wild fowl was knocked over on the beach, but no reliance could be put upon these sources of support. An expedition was accordingly made in the *Speedwell* to Banner Cove, in the hope of securing the provisions left in the *cache*, but two casks of biscuits were all that could now be found, and these were hardly got when the natives again gathered in force and compelled a hasty retreat.

The remaining months were months of dreadful suffer-

SEARCH AND DISCOVERY

ing. It had now become evident that food might utterly fail before any relief came. The outlook was dark indeed. Not only was starvation staring them in the face, but disease had laid its enervating hand upon every one of them. We can picture those weary men with each returning morning standing on the shore and scanning the horizon with anxious eyes, " waiting for the ship that never came, while the waves beat monotonously on the beach and the sea-birds screamed ominously overhead." And yet they seem never to have lost their courage or their faith. When the hope of life was gone they waited patiently for death, and when it came at last met it with cheerful resignation.

And now something must be said of the search for Gardiner and its results. H.M.S. *Dido* was not the first vessel to reach Banner Cove. The schooner *John Davidson*, under Captain W. H. Smyley, which had been hastily commissioned for the purpose in a South American port, arrived there on 21 October, 1851. No one was to be seen, but on the rocks at the entrance to the cove the words were painted:—

"DIG BELOW
GO TO SPANIARD HARBOUR
MARCH 1851"

Digging they found a note written by Captain Gardiner in which he said, "The Indians being so hostile, we have gone to Spaniard Harbour." Following these directions, Captain Smyley sailed to the place indicated, where, in his own words, he saw a sight that was "awful in the

VISIT OF THE "DIDO"

extreme.' In a stranded boat on the beach a dead body was lying; not far off was another washed to pieces by the waves; while yet a third lay half-buried in a shallow grave. One of the three was the surgeon, Mr. Williams; the other two were fishermen. No traces of Captain Gardiner and the rest were to be seen, and a heavy gale which sprang up all at once made it impossible to linger. Captain Smyley and his men had barely time to bury the dead on the beach in the teeth of a blinding snowstorm, and, as it was, experienced great difficulty in getting back to the schooner. They sailed at once for Monte Video with their dreadful news.

Next came the *Dido* from England. She too was guided from Banner Cove to Spaniard Harbour by the notice on the rocks, and her commander, setting to work with the energy and thoroughness characteristic of a British naval officer, succeeded in clearing up all that remained of the painful mystery. The body of Mr. Maidment was found in a cave to which direction was given by a hand painted on the rocks, with Psalm LXII. 5-8 painted underneath. The remains of Captain Gardiner himself were discovered by the side of a boat from which he seemed to have climbed out and been unable to get in again. For protection against the cold he had put on three suits of clothes and drawn woollen stockings over his arms above the other clothing. Below the waistcoat the seagulls had been at work, and had lessened the effects of corruption. His Bible was at hand, containing numberless underlined passages, many of which seemed to have been marked during the time of his suffering as peculiarly suited to his circumstances,

THE DIARY

Gardiner's journal was also found, carefully written up to the last, and giving many touching details of those dreadful months of starvation, disease, and slowly approaching death. Throughout all that period of anxiety and pain the strong faith of this heroic man appears to have burned like a lamp, while a spirit of affectionate brotherhood and quiet acceptance of the Divine will was displayed by every member of the doomed band. The Captain's last words seem to have been written when death was very near, and when his mind had begun to wander a little. He addresses himself to Mr. Williams—apparently forgetful of the fact (which is proved by his own journal) that the surgeon was already gone. The note is in pencil, written very indistinctly, and obliterated here and there.

"My dear Mr. Williams,—The Lord has seen fit to call home another of our little company. Our dear departed brother left the boat on Tuesday afternoon, and has not since returned. Doubtless he is in the presence of the Redeemer, Whom he served faithfully. Yet a little while, and though . . . the Almighty to sing the praises . . . throne. I neither hunger nor thirst, though five days without food. . . . Maidment's kindness to me . . . heaven.

"Your affectionate brother in . . .
"Allen F. Gardiner.
"September 6th, 1851."

Captain Morshead, of the *Dido*, gathered the remains together and buried them close to the cave in which the body of Mr. Maidment was found. The ship's

VICTORY THROUGH DEATH

flags hung at half-mast, one of the officers read the service for the dead, and three volleys of musketry were fired over the solitary grave.

Allen Gardiner's life is apt to strike us at first as one that was no less tragic in the fruitlessness of its great purpose than in the misery of its end. But it was not in vain that he strove, and, above all, it was not in vain that he and his brave comrades laid down their lives for Tierra del Fuego. The story of Captain Gardiner's death stirred England as he had never been able to stir her during his strenuous life. It gave a new impulse to the ideals which had led to the formation of the South American Missionary Society. It helped to bring about in due course, through the heroic labours of other noble men who took up the unfinished task, that complete transformation of the Fuegians to which reference was made in the beginning of this chapter. The people of Tierra del Fuego are no longer a degraded and cruel race, the terror of the sailor wrecked upon their dreary coasts. In every part of the archipelago to which the message of the Gospel has penetrated they are a humane and civilized folk, ready to give a kindly Christian welcome to any poor shipless mariner who has struggled to their shores out of the devouring waves.

LITERATURE.—*Hope Deferred, not Lost*, by the Rev. G. P. Despard, B.A. (South American Missionary Society); *From Cape Horn to Panama*, by Robert Young, F.R.S.G.S. (Simpkin, Marshall, Hamilton, Kent, and Co.); *Captain Allen Gardiner: Sailor and Saint*, by Jesse Page (S. W. Partridge and Co.); *Journal of Researches during the Voyage of H.M.S. Beagle*, by Charles Darwin (John Murray).

CHAPTER VII

THE SCHOONER OF KEPPEL ISLAND

A problem and a plan—The schooner—The island—Captain Gardiner's son—Jemmy Button—A disastrous enterprise—The massacre—Adventures of the ship's cook—Holding the fort—The new expedition—Forgiveness, not vengeance—Life on Keppel Island—The graves of the martyrs—Bishop Stirling and Ushuaia.

NOT long before the death of the heroic sailor who forms the subject of the preceding chapter, he drew up a plan for the future prosecution of the work to which he had devoted his life. He had learned by painful familiarity the difficulties and dangers which beset any attempt to settle at that time among a savage and unfriendly people in a barren and inhospitable land. Experience had shown him that there was a better way of attacking the problem of how to reach the inhabitants of Tierra del Fuego. And though he was not spared to make trial of that way himself, those who took up the task which death compelled him to lay down reaped the benefit of his hard-earned wisdom.

His plan in brief was this. The headquarters of the Mission should be transferred to one of the Falkland Islands, a lonely British group lying in the South Atlantic. some four or five hundred miles to the north-east of Cape Horn. To this station a few of the Fuegian natives

CAPTAIN GARDINER IN PERIL

Several war canoes full of armed Fuegians approached, and it was evident that nothing but dread of guns kept them from attacking instantly.

THE SCHOONER

should be taken in successive parties, so that the missionaries might have the double opportunity of acquiring their language and instructing them in Christian truth and the elements of a Christian civilization. As soon as sufficient progress had been made in both directions, a little vessel of about one hundred tons was to be built for the purpose of cruising about in the Straits of Magellan. It must be perfectly seaworthy, so as to face the fierce storms that rage around Cape Horn from the icy waters of the Antarctic Ocean. But it must also be fitted up internally in keeping with its character as a floating mission-house. In this way Captain Gardiner hoped that the problem which had baffled him so long would at last be solved.

When the news reached England of the dreadful calamity which had overtaken the founder of the South American Missionary Society and his whole party, the general feeling was that the brave seaman's hopes and plans were now buried with him for ever in his lonely grave. But it was not so. At a time when most of the supporters of the Society were crushed and dispirited, the honorary secretary, the Rev. G. P. Despard, uttered the noble words, "With God's help, the Mission shall be maintained." He aroused in many others a spirit of prayerful determination like his own, and before long Captain Gardiner's schemes began to be literally fulfilled. A stout little schooner, fitly called the *Allen Gardiner*, was launched at Dartmouth, and sailed from Bristol in 1855 with a fresh staff of missionaries. Keppel Island, one of the West Falklands, was secured from the British Government as a mission station. To crown the brightening prospects, Mr. Despard himself offered his services as

CAPTAIN GARDINER'S SON

superintendent of the Mission, and sailed for the Falklands with his own family and several additional helpers. Among these, it is interesting to note, was Mr. Allen W. Gardiner, demy of Magdalen College, Oxford, the only son of the departed hero.

The first work that faced the missionaries, on reaching the dreary uninhabited island which was to be their home, was the building of houses, the digging of peat for winter fuel, and the endeavour to contribute to their own maintenance by catching fish and birds for food and spearing seal for oil. It was a toilsome life they had to live, but not without variety. Every morning the men turned out at 6.30 to dig in the peat moss till breakfast-time. Each following hour of the day brought its appointed tasks. But when evening fell they gathered round their seal-oil lamps to study those languages which seemed most likely to fit them for the greater work to which they eagerly looked forward.

The first voyage which Mr. Despard made to Tierra del Fuego in the *Allen Gardiner* was chiefly important because it enabled the members of the new staff to see among the wild rocks of Spaniard Harbour the last resting-place of their seven predecessors. A pathetic feature of the cruise was the fact that Mr. Allen W. Gardiner was one of those on board. He kept a careful diary, some of the entries in which are particularly touching. Thus we find him, when the schooner is about to leave Spaniard Harbour, asking the captain for the gig and rowing himself ashore alone to take a last look, with what feelings we can imagine, at Pioneer Cavern and his father's grave.

JEMMY BUTTON

There was comparatively little intercourse with the natives on this first expedition to the islands, but better success attended a voyage in the following year. There was a well-known native at that period who had once been taken to England by a ship-captain, and had picked up a little English which he was always pleased to air before the sailors of any passing vessel. He had also acquired an English name, for he called himself Jemmy Button; while the little island on which he lived, and which lay off Woollya in the large island of Navarin, was known as Button Island.

In the hope of coming across Jemmy Button, the *Allen Gardiner* bore up for Woollya. It was a regular winter morning when they arrived, "snow lying on the deck and drifting into the sails and rigging, the wind fitful, howling, and gusty." Running for a cove abreast of Button Island, they found two canoes lying in shelter. One of the natives shouted out as the schooner approached, "Hillo, hoy, hoy!" which suggested that he might be the celebrated Button in person. But when the name "Jemmy Button" was shouted back, he only pointed to the island.

It was two days after, a lovely winter morning, with the sun shining brightly on the frosty ground and the high peaks of the mountains all dazzling white with snow, when four canoes were seen rounding the point of Button Island and coming across the sound. As soon as they were within hailing distance Mr. Gardiner sang out, "Jemmy Button," whereupon a man stood up in the foremost canoe and answered, "Yes, sir." In a few minutes Jemmy came up the ladder and shook hands, and was soon

THE BUTTON FAMILY

down in the cabin enjoying a breakfast of bread and butter with coffee. He seemed very frank, and gave his own people a good character, but mentioned that an English ship had fallen shortly before into the hands of an adjoining tribe, by whom every one of the crew was killed.

As Jemmy's command of a little English promised to be useful with a view to intercourse, he was asked if he would like to come with his wife and children to Keppel Island for several months. He was perfectly willing to do so, perhaps thinking that a course of English breakfasts would be a pleasant change from an unvarying diet of fish and seaweed. His family and he were accordingly given a passage to Keppel, the history of which as a mission station may now be said properly to begin.

The Buttons made themselves both agreeable and useful during their stay. Mrs. Despard speaks of Jemmy's great politeness, and tells how for any little trifle she might give him he would go and pick her a beautiful bouquet of wild flowers, or spear her a basket of fish. His eldest child also, to whom he had given the curious and unexplainable name of Threeboys, became a general favourite. But the family were of less service as instructors in the Fuegian language than had been expected. They did not like to speak their own tongue before the white strangers, and when they conversed with one another always did so in a whisper.

On his next voyage to Tierra del Fuego Mr. Despard took Jemmy Button, according to promise, back to the familiar life of the wigwam and the canoe. He had no difficulty, however, in persuading three other natives with

A DISASTROUS ENTERPRISE

their wives and children to return with him to the Falklands. These families stayed, as the Buttons had done, through the winter and spring, and delighted every one by their progress. Two lads named Okokko and Lucca seemed to be especially promising. They not only learned with ease to do a little carpentry, but appeared to understand all that was told them about God and Christ, and even began to give thanks at their meals and to pray at their bedside.

Forming his judgment of the Fuegian character from what he had seen of the natives at Keppel during months of close observation, Mr. Despard believed that the ferocity of the people must have been overstated, and that they could not be so bloodthirsty as they were commonly represented. He thought therefore that the first steps should now be taken towards establishing a missionary station in Tierra del Fuego itself, and he resolved to make a start at Woollya, the neighbourhood from which all his visitors had come. The enterprise was put into the hands of Mr. Phillips, one of the most trusted of the staff, and the *Allen Gardiner* sailed from Keppel Island for Woollya in the month of October, 1859.

Week after week passed away, and there was no sign of the returning vessel. At length Mr. Despard grew so anxious that he made his way to Stanley, the chief port of the Falklands, and engaged Captain Smyley, of the schooner *Nancy*, to sail at once on a voyage of inquiry.

It was not long before Captain Smyley returned with news not less terrible than that which he had been the

THE MASSACRE

first to bring eight years before regarding the fate of Captain Gardiner and his party. The natives at Woollya had massacred Mr. Phillips, Captain Fell of the *Allen Gardiner*, and six others. Of the whole company on board the schooner only one had escaped. From this man, who had been the ship's cook, the following narrative was obtained.

When the *Allen Gardiner* reached Woollya, the people appeared perfectly friendly, and for several days a good deal of intercourse went freely on between the vessel and the shore. Sunday coming round, a landing was made on the island with the view of conducting Christian worship in the presence of the natives, only the cook being left on board in charge.

For a time everything seemed to go well. But suddenly a concerted rush was made upon the white men and all were barbarously murdered. Not a hand or a voice was raised in their defence, though the cook saw the lad Okokko running up and down the beach in evident distress. We can imagine the feelings of that solitary watcher on the schooner's deck as he gazed with horror-stricken eyes on the dreadful scene which was enacted on the shore a few hundred yards from where he stood. With a sense of absolute powerlessness to help them, he saw all his companions brutally done to death, and he knew that his own turn would come next unless he could make his escape before the savages, now drunk with blood, attacked the vessel.

Realizing that now or never was his chance, he slid down into a boat, and rowing with all haste to the shore, disappeared in the depths of the dense forest before his

ADVENTURES OF THE SHIP'S COOK

red-handed pursuers could overtake him. In these forest depths he lay hid for several days, till at length hunger and cold drove him out among the natives. By this time their passion for blood seemed to have been sated, and though he got rough treatment from some of them, others supplied him with food and showed him a little kindness until the arrival of the *Nancy* placed him once more in the midst of friends.

Meanwhile the *Allen Gardiner* had been completely ransacked and plundered, but not burnt or otherwise destroyed, and Captain Smyley was able to convey her back to the Falkland Islands in safety. He brought along with him the lad Okokko and his wife Camilenna, who were very earnest in their entreaties to be removed from their barbarous surroundings and taken back once more to their Christian friends at Keppel Island.

Thus, what may be called the first chapter in the strange romance of a missionary schooner closed in a scene of tragedy and blood. It was more than three years before the *Allen Gardiner* sailed to Tierra del Fuego again.

The next voyage of the schooner was to England, to which Mr. Despard now returned, leaving two missionaries to hold the fort in Keppel Island until better days should come. One of these was William Bartlett, who had charge of the Mission farm. The other was Mr. Bridges, Mr. Despard's adopted son, a young man of a very fine spirit and possessed of a rare faculty for language. To him more than to any other the missionaries owed their eventual mastery of the difficult Fuegian tongue—an acquirement which smoothed away many

—114—

HOLDING THE FORT

obstacles and misunderstandings. In the care of the Mission property, in the further instruction of Okokko and Camilenna, and in the task of learning not only to speak Fuegian, but how to reduce it to a grammar, these two brave men whiled away the lonely months and years of waiting.

After two such crushing blows as had now fallen upon the South American Society within the space of eight years, it might almost be supposed that any idea of converting the Fuegians would be finally abandoned. But the patient heroism of the founder had become part of the Society's inheritance, and there was no slackening in the determination to go on. The story of some Missions is inspiring because of the vast and striking results which are achieved. There was no possibility of vast results among the scanty and dwindling tribes of a desolate archipelago. But this only makes us admire the more the undaunted courage and unfaltering perseverance of those who, in the face of one terrible disaster after another, still took for their motto, "With God's help, the Mission shall be maintained."

With a view to increasing both her seaworthiness and her accommodation, the *Allen Gardiner* was now lengthened, and thereafter this historic schooner sailed from Bristol once again, with a fresh missionary party, to resume her work in the icy Southern seas. The leader of the enterprise on this occasion was the well-known Mr. Stirling, who seven years afterwards was consecrated as the first Bishop of the Falkland Islands.

The plans of the Society as well as its schooner had now been enlarged. Its operations were about to be

THE NEW EXPEDITION

extended northwards along the South American coast until they should reach from Cape Horn to Panama. Tierra del Fuego, however, still remained the special objective of the *Allen Gardiner*, and one of Mr. Stirling's earliest duties was to reopen that communication with the natives which had ceased after the massacre of 1859. He was greatly assisted in this task by both Mr. Bridges and Okokko, for the former had now become quite an expert in Fuegian, while the latter could speak English very well. As the schooner sailed about among the islands, the missionaries by means of these two highly competent interpreters made their friendly intentions everywhere known. At Woollya they were received with some suspicion, for the people there, recognizing the vessel, thought not unnaturally that it had come back now on a mission of vengeance. But when persuaded that their crime had been forgiven, and that Mr. Stirling and his companions had no thoughts towards them but thoughts of peace, they became quite enthusiastic, and far more of them volunteered to come to Keppel Island than could possibly be accommodated there. The chief difficulty now was to select from among the applicants those who were most likely to be of use in furthering the aims of the Mission.

The change for the natives from Tierra del Fuego to the Falklands was, no doubt, great. At home their time was largely spent in paddling about in their frail canoes. They lived mainly on fish, which they speared with great dexterity, their only vegetable diet being seaweed from the rocks, or fungi, which grew plentifully on the rugged hills. One of the occasional excitements of existence came

LIFE ON KEPPEL ISLAND

from the arrival of a shoal of whales. They did not venture to attack those monsters of the deep in the open sounds, but they were frequently indebted to the fierce swordfish, which would so harass the clumsy creatures that they floundered into the shallows and got stranded; and then the hungry and watchful Indians had their chance.

At Keppel Island the Fuegians had to live a life that was much more civilized. They were expected to attend at Christian worship every day, and the younger members of the community were taught the elements of an ordinary education; but they were not asked to live after a fashion which would have been quite unnatural for them, as it was recognized that allowance and provision must be made for their hereditary instincts. And so, while they were trained to habits of industry in the Mission gardens and the peat valley, they still enjoyed the pleasures of spearing fish, as well as the novel and to them most exhilarating excitement of chasing the cattle, which were bred on the Mission farm, but allowed to run in a wild state over the island. It shows the deep-seated impulses of the natural man that even those who had stayed for a period at the station, and had learned to appreciate the comforts of a settled life and the blessings of Christianity, were generally quite glad by and by to go back to their own people. Their minds were now uplifted and enlarged, but they still loved the old, familiar, adventurous canoe life among the creeks and sounds of the Magellan Straits.

Some time after the arrival of Mr. Stirling the growing confidence inspired by the missionaries received a striking illustration. On one of the cruises of the *Allen Gardiner*

THE GRAVES OF THE MARTYRS

the natives of Woollya of their own accord pointed out the spot where they had laid the bodies of the eight men whom they had murdered in November, 1859. They had carefully carried them to a quiet place among the rocks and covered them with large stones to keep them from being eaten by the foxes: and here ever since in their rocky sepulchres they had been lying undisturbed. Two of the bodies—those of Mr. Phillips and Captain Fell—could still be identified quite unmistakably. All were reverently lifted and buried in a Christian grave, with the simple and beautiful rites of the Church of England. The collect for St. Stephen's Day was most appropriately read, with its reference to the first Christian martyr and his prayer for those who murdered him. The schooner's flag meanwhile hung half-mast high, and at the close of the service two signal guns, booming across the water and echoing from rock to rock, announced to the company of Christian mourners and awestruck natives that all was over.

Year after year the *Allen Gardiner* continued to go forth on her blessed work, bringing successive batches of natives to Keppel, and taking them back again after a while to their wild homes to act the part of the leaven in the midst of the meal. And at last in 1869 a mission station was opened by Mr. Stirling in person at Ushuaia, some distance to the west of Spaniard Harbour, sacred to the memory of Captain Gardiner, and on the south coast of the main island of Tierra del Fuego. Here for seven months Mr. Stirling lived in a little hut, before which he often paced up and down as the shadows of evening were falling upon sea and mountain, feeling, he tells us, as if he were

BISHOP STIRLING AND USHUAIA

"a sentinel stationed at the southernmost outpost of God's great army."

From this remotest outpost of the Church of Christ he was summoned suddenly to England to be consecrated Bishop of the Falkland Islands, with a diocese which included practically the whole of the South American continent. The work he had begun in Ushuaia was taken up by Mr. Bridges and others, and when Bishop Stirling next saw the place in 1872 it was a little Christian settlement that lay before him. Stirling House, the iron house of the Mission, occupied a conspicuous position, while around it were the wigwams and cultivated gardens of a native colony. A little chapel showed the consecration of the whole to God, and in that chapel on the Lord's Day the Bishop joined with Mr. Bridges—now an ordained clergyman—in administering the sacrament of Baptism to thirty-six Fuegians, adult and infant, and in joining seven couples in Christian marriage.

A genuine reformation in the Fuegian character had now begun. That for which, first, Captain Gardiner and his whole party, and at a later date Mr. Phillips and Captain Fell, with six other gallant men, had laid down their lives was already in process of accomplishment. The brutal natives of the Archipelago were being transformed into the likeness of peaceable Christian men and women. The best, because the most disinterested proof of this is found in a British Admiralty chart of 1871. In this chart the attention of mariners passing through the Straits of Magellan is directed to the existence of the mission station of Ushuaia; and they are assured that within a radius of thirty miles no shipwrecked crew need expect other

SOURCES OF THE NARRATIVE

than kindly treatment from any natives into whose hands they may fall.

For the foregoing narrative the author is indebted to *The Story of Commander Allen Gardiner*, R.N., by the Rev. John W. Marsh, M.A., and the Rev. W. H. Stirling, D.D., Bishop of the Falkland Islands (James Nisbet and Co.), and also to Mr. Marsh's *First Fruits of the South American Mission*, which was kindly lent him by the Secretaries of the Society.

OCEANIA

CHAPTER VIII

THE MARTYR-BISHOP OF MELANESIA

In the Eton playing-fields—A case of moral courage—Bishop Selwyn and Coley Patteson—Selwyn's work in Melanesia—Wanted a helper!—The helper found—Patteson as skipper and college tutor—As Bishop of Melanesia—Exciting adventnres—The kidnappers—The Bishop's death.

THE Duke of Wellington used to be credited with the striking remark, "The battle of Waterloo was won in the playing-fields of Eton." Like many other memorable sayings which have been attributed to great men, this one is now generally believed to be apocryphal. Nevertheless, in its own paradoxical and exaggerated way, it embodies a truth, the truth being that the boy is "the father of the man," and that the victories of after years find their explanation in the qualities of strength and courage and manly endurance which have been worked into the character when life was young. The hero of the following story happens to have been an Eton boy, and one who greatly distinguished himself among his companions in the Eton playing-fields.

—121—

COLEY PATTESON

And no one who reads the story of his life can fail to see that the schoolboy was the father of the missionary, that it was the same qualities of athletic vigour, of enthusiasm, of moral strength by which Coley Patteson was marked out at Eton College that gained him his place of renown in the history of missions as the apostle and martyr of Melanesia.

John Coleridge Patteson, Coley Patteson, as he was familiarly called, was the son of Mr. Justice Patteson, a distinguished lawyer in his time, and the grand-nephew of the poet Coleridge. As a boy he was especially distinguished for his physical prowess, which raised him ultimately to the coveted position of captain of the Eton Eleven. Once, in the annual match with Harrow at Lord's, it was Patteson who won the game for his school by putting on fifty runs and completely breaking the neck of the Harrow bowling. On another occasion, in a game at Eton, he so persistently defied the bowling of Lillywhite, the famous professional, that the latter became quite irritated and said, " Mr. Patteson, I should like to bowl to you on Lord's ground, and it would be different." It was characteristic of young Patteson's modesty to reply at once, "Oh, of course ; I know you would have me out directly there."

But this brilliant Eton cricketer had other qualities which do not always accompany athletic distinction. He was a quick and diligent scholar, especially strong in languages, a fact which stood him in good stead when he came to move about in a scattered archipelago, almost every island of which had its own separate dialect. Better still, he was a lad of fearless moral courage.

A CASE OF MORAL COURAGE

While up to any amount of fun, ready to sing his song at a cricket or football supper as mirthfully as the most lighthearted of the party, he could not tolerate any kind of coarseness or indecency. At the annual dinner of the Eton Eleven the custom had grown up of allowing rather objectionable songs to be given. After Coley Patteson had passed into the Eleven he was present at a dinner when one of the boys began to sing a ditty of a decidedly questionable character. At once Coley called out, "If that does not stop, I shall leave the room"; and as the singer went on, he jumped up and went out. His next step was to intimate to the captain that unless an apology was made he would leave the Eleven. Knowing that he could not dispense with so brilliant a bat, the captain compelled the offender to apologize; and during the rest of Coley Patteson's time at Eton no more songs of that kind were sung at the annual dinner.

It was while Coley was at Eton, and when he was about fourteen years of age, that a vision of what was to be the great work of his life first dawned upon him. In the parish church of Windsor, one Sunday afternoon, he heard a missionary sermon from Bishop Selwyn of New Zealand, a diocese which at that time included the Melanesian Islands, and he was deeply touched by the Bishop's appeal for help. Not long afterwards in his father's house he met Bishop Selwyn face to face. The Bishop, who was just about to leave England for the South Seas, turned to the boy's mother and said, half in playfulness, half in earnest, "Lady Patteson, will you give me Coley?" From that day forward, deep down in the heart of the lad, there lived the

BISHOP SELWYN

thought of some day joining the heroic Bishop of New Zealand in his pioneer work among the islanders of the Pacific.

But something must now be said about Melanesia and Bishop Selwyn. When the see of New Zealand was first formed the Bishop was entrusted with the care of the innumerable islands dispersed in various groups over the South Pacific. The interest of the Church of England in the islanders, however, had been anticipated by the zeal of other Churches or missionary societies. The Wesleyans were at work in the Fiji Islands, the Presbyterians in the New Hebrides, the London Missionary Society, ever since the time of John Williams, in Polynesia. There still remained farther to the west, and forming a far-off fringe along the south-eastern coast of New Guinea and the north-eastern coast of Australia, the Melanesian or Black Island group, so called because the inhabitants are darker-skinned than the other Pacific races and appear to have a good deal of the negro in their composition.

Bishop Selwyn very wisely resolved that, to prevent overlapping of missionary effort and consequent confusion of the native mind, he would confine his attentions to these Melanesians, and he entered into his labours among them with all the ardour and heroism of the true pioneer. Like his future colleague Coleridge Patteson, he was a distinguished athlete. He had rowed in the first Inter-University Boat Race in 1829, and was further a spendid pedestrian and a magnificent swimmer. In his work in Melanesia all these powers came into full play. There was nothing of the conventional bishop about his outward

SELWYN'S WORK IN MELANESIA

appearance or manner of life. His usual way of landing on an island was to take a header from a boat which lay off at a safe distance, and swim ashore through the surf. When hard manual work had to be done, he was the first to set the example. If dangers had to be met, he did not hesitate to face them. If hardships had to be borne, he bore them cheerfully. Once, for instance, when an inhospitable chief refused him the shelter of a hut, he retired to a pig-stye and spent the night there in patience and content. How versatile he was may be judged from an instance like the following. On one occasion he had undertaken by request to convey to New Zealand in his missionary schooner a Melanesian chief's daughter and her attendant native girl. The pair were dressed according to the ideas of propriety which prevailed in the islands, but were hardly presentable in a British colony. The Bishop spent much of his time on the voyage in manufacturing to the best of his ability out of his own counterpane two petticoats for the dark maidens. And so attractive did he make the garments, with their trimmings of scarlet ribbon, that the girls were as delighted to put them on as the Bishop was anxious that they should do so.

One of the great difficulties of the work in Melanesia sprang from the endless varieties of dialects which were employed. Bishop Selwyn conceived the plan of persuading native youths from the different islands to come with him to New Zealand to undergo there a course of instruction and training which would fit them for Christian work among their own people when they returned. But if this plan was to be carried out efficiently there was need of

WANTED A HELPER!

assistance, and such assistance as was required was by no means easy to find. The man wanted must be possessed of physical hardihood, ready and fit to "rough it," as the Bishop himself did while cruising among the islands. But he must also be a man of culture and character, to whom the difficult task of educating the native youths could be safely entrusted.

In search of such a helper as this Bishop Selwyn eventually paid a visit to England. Thirteen years had passed since he had stirred the missionary instinct in young Patteson's soul by saying to his mother in his hearing, "Will you give me Coley?" Neither the Bishop nor the boy had forgotten the incident. But Coley meanwhile had passed through Oxford and become curate of Alfington, in the parish of Ottery St. Mary. His mother was dead, his father now an old man in poor health. A strong sense of filial love and duty had hitherto kept him from the thought of leaving home so long as his father was alive. But Bishop Selwyn came to see Sir John Patteson and Coley, and set the claims of Melanesia before them in such a way that both father and son realized that they must not hesitate to make the needful sacrifice of affection. That sacrifice was soon made. When the Bishop sailed again for his far-off Pacific see, Coleridge Patteson stood beside him on the deck as his devoted follower and brother missionary.

As Patteson knew that his work would largely consist in sailing about among the islands, he applied himself busily throughout the long ocean voyage not only to the task of mastering the native languages under the Bishop's tuition, but to a careful study under the captain of the

PATTESON AS SKIPPER

art of navigation. He soon became an expert shipmaster, so that he was able by and by to navigate the *Southern Cross*, the little missionary schooner, on her various voyages through dangerous seas.

Arriving in New Zealand, he speedily had a taste of the kind of life that was in store for him. His immediate work lay in the College which had been established for the native youths, but he had to be ready, just as Bishop Selwyn himself was, to turn his hand to any kind of duty. In one of his letters he tells how, as the two were superintending the landing of their goods from a vessel by means of carts, the tide being very low, three of the horses got into water which was rather deep for them, and were in danger of being drowned. In a moment the two missionaries had their coats off and their trousers rolled up, and had plunged in to the rescue, splashing about in the muddy water in full view of the crowd on the beach. " This is your first lesson in mud-larking, Coley," remarked the Bishop, as they emerged at length wet and dirty, and laughing at each other's appearance.

But Patteson's special task was, as he put it himself, " to rove about the Melanesian department," and for several years he spent half of his time at sea. Fortunately he was a good sailor, and in every way worthy to be the skipper of the *Southern Cross*. He took thorough delight in his work, enjoying its romantic aspects, but still more feeling the privilege of carrying the Gospel of Christ to men and women who had never heard it before, and who needed it very sadly. On his early cruises he was accompanied by the Bishop, and their most frequent method of landing at any island to which they came was to plunge

HORRORS OF CANNIBALISM

into the sea in light suits which they wore for the purpose, and make for the crowd of armed natives who were sure to be standing on the beach. Sometimes they were in danger, but firmness and kindness and tact carried them through, and in not a few cases they were able to persuade a chief to allow his son, or some other promising youth, to return with them to New Zealand to join the other young men who were receiving at the College the elements of a Christian education.

So friendly was their reception for the most part, that Patteson was inclined to scoff at the notion of describing these gentle-looking people as savages at all. "Savages are all Fridays," he wrote, "if you know how to treat them." But at times he was inclined to carry his confidence in them too far, and it was well for him in those early days that he had the Bishop at hand, who had learned by experience the need for perpetual caution. For there were plenty of real savages in Melanesia, and now and then there came sharp reminders of the fact. At one island, where they were received with every sign of friendliness and conducted to the chief's long hut, they saw hanging from the roof a row of human skulls, some of them black with soot, others so white that it was evident they had been quite lately added to the collection. In another place, while passing through some bush, they came upon the remains of human bodies, relics of a recent cannibal feast. Occasionally, too, as they swam away from what had seemed to be a friendly crowd, an arrow or two whizzed past their heads, showing that they had left some ill-disposed persons behind them. One island that they visited in safety they knew to have been the scene

BISHOP OF MELANESIA

some time before of a deed of blood of which the crew of a British vessel were the victims. Their ship had struck upon the reef, and when they got ashore the natives killed the whole ship's company of them, nineteen in all. Ten of these the cannibals ate on the spot; the remaining nine they sent away as presents to their friends.

A voyage over, and the chief fruits of the cruise gathered together, in the persons of a number of bright lads who had been persuaded to become scholars, Patteson would settle down for some months to play another rôle, that of a college tutor, but under circumstances very different from any that the name is apt to suggest. He had to teach his pupils everything, not only reading, writing, arithmetic, and the elements of Christian truth, but how to sweep their rooms and make their beds, how to print and weave and saw and build. Lessons in school over, his old proficiency at cricket became useful once more, and the former captain of the Eton Eleven might be seen patiently coaching his young barbarians, until they caught something of the English skill and enthusiasm in the great English game.

At length after six years of strenuous apprenticeship to the work of a pioneer missionary in the Pacific, there came a great change in Coleridge Patteson's position. Bishop Selwyn had long been convinced of the necessity of forming Melanesia into a separate diocese, and had come to recognize not less clearly the pre-eminent fitness of Mr. Patteson to occupy the new see. The representations he made to the home authorities on this subject were successful, and in 1861 Coley Patteson became Bishop of Melanesia at the early age of thirty-three.

EXCITING ADVENTURES

His elevation made little difference, however, either in the general character of his work or in his manner of doing it. He cruised about among the islands as before—dressed commonly in an old flannel shirt, and trousers somewhat the worse for wear—a handy costume for one who had constantly to do a good deal of swimming and wading. His voyages as Bishop, at the same time, were on a wider scale than any he had attempted formerly, for he felt his larger responsibilities, and tried to reach even those islands which had hitherto been regarded as inaccessible.

Several times he had very narrow escapes. Once in particular, when he had gone ashore at a place where the natives made a show of friendship, he discovered from their conversation and gestures as soon as they had him in their power that it was their deliberate intention to kill him. The reason, he found afterwards, was that one of their friends had been murdered by a white trader, and with a savage sense of justice they felt that they were entitled to this white man's life. The Bishop knew that humanly speaking he had no chance of mercy, but he begged permission to be allowed to pray, and kneeling down he committed his soul to God. The natives did not understand a single word that he uttered, but the look they saw in his face as he knelt so impressed and overawed them that they said to one another, "He does not look like a murderer." And as soon as he was done, with many signs of courtesy they conducted him back to the beach again and bade him farewell.

On another occasion, in connexion with a later cruise, a sad incident took place at the island of Santa Cruz. The

A SHOWER OF ARROWS

natives here showed no signs of opposition when he landed, but after he had returned to his boat and pushed off, a shower of arrows was discharged from the beach. The Bishop, who was at the stern, unshipped the rudder and held it up as a shield to try to ward off the deadly shafts. In spite of his efforts three of the party, all of them Christian young men, were transfixed. Fortunately the arrows were not poisoned, as Melanesian arrows often were, but Patteson had great difficulty in extracting them. In one case he found it quite impossible to draw out the arrowhead from a man's wrist, and was obliged to pull it from the other side right through his arm. This poor fellow took lock-jaw, and died in a few days, after dreadful agonies of pain.

For ten strenuous years after his consecration as Bishop, Patteson sailed to and fro among the Melanesian Islands. Sometimes, through illness and weakness, brought on by the constant strain, he was in great suffering; but he never ceased to rejoice in his work. At last, however, a dark shadow fell across his path, a shadow which deepened to the awful tragedy of his death.

The traders of the Pacific had discovered that it was more remunerative to kidnap natives, clap them under hatches, and sail with them as virtual slaves to the plantations of Queensland or Fiji, than to busy themselves in collecting sandal-wood or copra for the legitimate market. Not a few of them had entered into this unscrupulous and vile traffic, which soon produced an unpleasant change all over the islands in the attitude of the natives to white men.

BISHOP PATTESON DEFENDING HIMSELF AND HIS MEN
WITH A RUDDER

They were attacked by the natives of Santa Cruz just after they had pushed off from the shore. Fortunately the arrows were not poisonous, but one of the natives died of his wounds.

THE KIDNAPPERS

Worse still, some of these kidnappers used Patteson's name as a decoy. Coming to an island where he was known and trusted, they would tell the people that the Bishop was on board and wanted to see them. In some cases they even went the length of making an effigy of him, dressed in a black coat and holding a Bible in his hands; and this they placed in a position where it could be seen by those ashore. When the unsuspecting blacks came off in their canoes and climbed on board, they were quickly tumbled down into the hold among the other miserable wretches who were imprisoned there.

These were the malign influences which led to the murder of Bishop Patteson. He is the Martyr of Melanesia, but it was the kidnapping traders more than the ill-used natives who were responsible for his death.

It was on a day of September, 1871, that the *Southern Cross* stood off the coral reef of the island of Nukapu. Several canoes were seen cruising about, apparently in a state of some excitement. The Bishop entered the schooner's boat and pulled towards the reef, but the tide was too low for the boat to get across. At this juncture two natives approached, and proposed to take the Bishop into their light canoe and paddle him over the reef to the shore. He at once consented. The boat's crew saw him land safely on the beach, but after that lost sight of him.

For about half an hour the boat had been lying-to and waiting, when from several canoes, which had gradually been drawing near, a shower of arrows fell upon the crew. They pulled back immediately in great haste, and were soon out of range, but not till three persons had been

THE BISHOP'S DEATH

struck with poisoned arrows, two of whom, the **Rev.** Joseph Atkins and a Christian native, subsequently died.

When the tide rose high enough to make it possible for the boat to cross the barrier reef, it was dispatched from the schooner, in the hope of getting some intelligence about the Bishop. As the men pulled across the lagoon towards the shore two canoes put off to meet them. One cast off the other and went back, the one which was left drifting towards them as they approached.

As it came near they noticed what looked like a bundle lying in the bottom, and when they drew alongside they saw that this was the dead Bishop, lying there with a calm smile on his upturned face. His body was wrapped in a native mat, and over his breast there lay a leaf of the cocoa-nut palm, with five knots tied in the long sprays. What those mysterious knots meant was partly explained when the mat was unwrapped and five deadly wounds, inflicted with club, spear, and arrows, were discovered on the body.

It was afterwards learned that five Nukapu natives had been stolen by the kidnappers. The islanders doubtless looked upon them as having been murdered, and so their nearest relatives, exercising the old tribal right of exacting "blood for blood," had stained their weapons one by one in the blood of the white Bishop, who was thus called upon to lay down his life for the sins of his own unworthy fellow-countrymen.

The people of Nukapu have long since repented of their crime. On the spot where the Bishop fell there now

A SIMPLE MEMORIAL

stands, by their own desire, a simple but impressive cross with this inscription upon it:—

In Memory of
John Coleridge Patteson, D.D.,
Missionary Bishop,
Whose life was here taken by men for whom he would
gladly have given it.

The authoritative source for Bishop Selwyn's life is the biography by Rev. H. W. Tucker, and for Bishop Patteson's, *The Life of John Coleridge Patteson*, by Miss C. M. Yonge (Macmillan and Co.). Mention should also be made of *Bishop Patteson*, by J. Page (S. W. Partridge and Co.), which is an excellent popular narrative.

CHAPTER IX

ONE OF THE UNRETURNING BRAVE

An unexplored island—"Tamate"—Sea-dwellings and tree-dwellings—A ghastly parcel—Toeless feet—A perilous retreat—Dangers of the surf—Chalmers as a great explorer—As a teacher of the A B C—R. L. Stevenson and Tamate—The last expedition to the Fly River.

THERE are persons of a romantic turn who sometimes lament the rapidity and thoroughness with which the work of civilization is being carried on. Steamships, they remind us, now ply up and down the waters of the great lakes of Central Africa, and right through the heart of the Dark Continent a railway is being steadily pushed on. There are places to which a generation ago it would have taken much more than a year to send a message from London or Edinburgh, whereas now to those same places a message can be sent and an answer received in less than twelve hours. The North Pole, we have seen it affirmed, is now almost the only place left to be discovered on the face of the globe, so that whenever Dr. Nansen or Lieutenant Peary, or some other Arctic hero, has succeeded in realizing his ambition, whether by dog-sledge or airship or submarine, it will be necessary for would-be explorers to sit down, like Alexander the

AN UNEXPLORED ISLAND

Great, and weep because there are no more worlds to conquer.

But the earth is by no means so tame and familiar a planet as these persons imagine. It is only want of knowledge that will make us speak as if hardly any part of the globe still remains unknown. In Asia and Africa, in South America and Australia, there are still large tracts of territory which the foot of civilized man has never yet trod. And there is an island in the southern seas which, if judged by its size, would have to be described as the most important island in the world, and yet, of all the world's larger islands, it is precisely the one regarding which our knowledge is most incomplete.

Papua, or New Guinea, the island to which we refer, lies to the north-east of the Australian continent, separated from it by the Torres Straits, only eighty miles across. In shape it resembles one of the huge Saurian reptiles of a prehistoric era; and, if we may carry out this comparison in describing its size, it may be added that from head to tail it measures 1490 miles in length, while it is 430 miles in breadth across the thickest part of its body. Covering as it does an area of considerably more than 300,000 square miles, it is quite six times the size of England. Its chief river, the Fly, is tidal at a distance of 130 miles from the sea, and has been navigated by steamer for over 600 miles of its course. The island can boast of a mighty range of mountains quite worthy to be compared to the Alps, the loftiest peak, indeed, rising nearer to the sky than the white dome of Mont Blanc.

Of the people of this great island, however, hardly anything was known thirty years ago, except that they were warlike cannibals, whose only regular trade was to barter sago for earthenware pots in which to cook man. To Port Moresby, on the south-east coast of this mysterious and dreaded land, there came in 1876 James Chalmers, or "Tamate," an agent of the London Missionary Society. Combining, as he did in a very unusual degree, the qualities of missionary and explorer, he soon greatly increased our knowledge of the geography of New Guinea and of the superstitions, habits, and social customs of its various and widely differing tribes.

Chalmers was no inexperienced tyro of the South Seas when he first arrived at Port Moresby to enter upon that career of constant adventure by land and sea, on the rivers and in the forests, with Papuan savages or with the Papuan surf, in which the next twenty-five years of his life were to be spent. He had already been shipwrecked on a coral-reef in the *John Williams*, the London Missionary Society's vessel, named after that splendid hero of Polynesia whose true successor Chalmers himself became. He had gone with his young wife on a voyage of 2000 miles in the brig of "Bully Hayes," the notorious pirate of the Pacific, and had so fascinated that ferocious nineteenth-century buccaneer that he behaved to his unwonted passengers like a perfect gentleman. He had spent ten years on Rarotonga, among the former cannibals of that beautiful coral island. It was from the Rarotongans that he got the name "Tamate," which stuck to him for the rest of his life, though it was nothing else than the result of an ineffectual native attempt to pronounce the Scottish name of "Chalmers." In Rarotonga Tamate had gained much valuable experience; but the restless spirit of the

A Native Village in New Guinea. The Houses are all built on Piles driven into the Ground

TREE-DWELLINGS

pioneer was in his blood, and it was a joyful day for him when word came from London that he was to proceed to New Guinea to enter upon what he felt from the first to be the true work of his life.

The people of New Guinea are sprung from various original stocks, and are broken up besides into numerous isolated tribes which differ greatly from one another in colour, feature, and language. But Chalmers found that, in addition to this, every village formed a community by itself, living at enmity with its neighbours and in constant suspicion of them. The best proof of this was afforded by the construction of the houses, built as they invariably were with a view to protection against sudden attack. Along the coast marine villages were common, Port Moresby itself being an example. The houses in this case were counterparts of the lake-dwellings of primitive man in European countries, being erected on tall piles driven into the sea-bottom at such a distance from the shore that a small steamer was able to thread its way between the houses, and even to anchor safely in the main street. Inland villages, similarly, were built on poles which projected not less than ten feet above the ground, access to the platform on which a house stood being obtained by means of a ladder. Among the hill-tribes, again, tree-dwellings were most common, these being particularly inaccessible and thus most easy to defend. On his first arrival at Port Moresby, Chalmers took a long walk inland till he was about 1100 feet above sea-level, and found houses built not only on the summit of a mountain ridge, but on the tops of the very highest trees that were growing there.

CRUISE ALONG THE SOUTH COAST

Tamate at once set himself to acquire some knowledge of his vast diocese and to win the confidence of the natives. He had all the qualities for the work that lay before him. He could navigate a whale-boat through the heavy surf which crashes along the level coasts, as if bred to the job. And at tramping through the forests or climbing the mountains no one could beat him; though he confesses to sometimes having sore feet, and expresses the wicked wish that shoemakers could be compelled to wear the boots they send out to missionaries. As for the natives, he won them by a kind of personal fascination he had which was felt by every one who met him—man-eating savage or missionary-loving old lady, a piratical outlaw like "Bully Hayes," or a literary dreamer and critic like Robert Louis Stevenson. Unarmed but fearless, Tamate never hesitated to walk right into the midst of a crowd of armed and threatening cannibals. For the most part he won their friendship at the first meeting without difficulty, though every now and then he came across some troublesome customers and had a narrow escape with his life.

One of Chalmers' earliest expeditions was a cruise along the south coast from east to west, in the course of which he visited 105 villages, 90 of which had never seen a white man before. Being new to the country, he met with much to surprise or amuse him. The Papuans are passionately fond of pigs, especially when roasted; but it astonished their visitor to find that they preserved the skulls of dead pigs in their houses along with those of their departed relatives, and still more to see a woman nursing her baby at one breast and a young pig at the other. One day

"I Entered that Eerie Place"

The holiest place of a New Guinea temple. Chalmers entered it alone; the chief who had accompanied him so far was too frightened to go further. It contained six strange figures with enormous frog-like mouths out of which small bats flew in rapid succession.

A GHASTLY PARCEL

when he had taken his seat in the middle of a native house, right in front of the fire, and was busy tracing his course on a chart, he began to wonder how it was that strange dark drops kept falling all around him and sometimes on the chart itself. When he looked up the reason became apparent. A recently deceased grandmother had been made up into a bulky parcel and hung from the roof right above the fire, with a view to being thoroughly smoked and dried. Tamate's shout of disgust brought in the owner of the house, who hastily took down his late grandmother and walked off with her on his shoulder, to deposit her elsewhere until the departure of this too fastidious traveller.

But if Chalmers was sometimes astonished at first by the Papuans and their ways, the astonishment was by no means altogether upon his side. His white skin was a source of perpetual wonder, especially if he had occasion to roll up his sleeves or change his shirt, and so exposed parts of his body that were not so bronzed as his cheeks by the sea air and the burning sun. Great, too, was the perplexity caused by his combination of a white face with black and toeless feet—perplexity which suddenly turned into horror if he lifted his legs and pulled off his boots.

These, however, were among the lighter phases of his experiences as a pioneer. Until he became known, along many a league of coast and in the deep recesses of the forest, as the best friend of the Papuan people, Tamate had constantly to face death in the grimmest forms, and with a vision of the cannibal cooking-pot lying ever in the background. Here is a hairbreadth escape which

A PERILOUS RETREAT

looks thrilling enough as we read it in his *Adventures in New Guinea*, though it does not seem half so dramatic on the printed page as it did when the present writer heard Tamate relate it himself—"a big, stout, wildish-looking man," as R. L. Stevenson described him, "with big bold black eyes," which glowed and flashed as he told his story and suited the action to the word.

On one of his coasting voyages in the *Ellengowan*, a little steamer that belonged to the Mission, he came to a bay in which he had never been before. He put off for the shore as soon as possible, but the moment his boat touched the beach he was surrounded by a threatening crowd of natives, every one of them armed with club or spear. The savages absolutely forbade him to land, but he sprang ashore notwithstanding, followed by the mate of the *Ellengowan*, a fine, daring fellow with something of Tamate's own power of feeling least fear where most danger seemed to be. Up the long sea-beach the two men walked, accompanied by the hostile crowd, till they came to what was evidently the house of the village chief. The old man sat in solemn dignity on the raised platform in front of his house, and did not condescend to take the least notice of his visitors. Climbing up to the platform, Tamate laid down some presents he had brought, but the surly magnate flung them back in his face. It now became apparent that a row was brewing, for the crowd took its cue from the chief, and was beginning to jostle rudely and to indulge in bursts of brutal laughter. Turning to the mate, who stood a little way behind, Tamate asked him in English how things looked. "Bad, sir," he replied; "the bush is full of natives, and there are arms

A CRITICAL MOMENT

Chalmers was followed by a big and angry crowd. One savage with a large club walked immediately behind him. Chalmers felt that he must have that club or it would have him, so taking a piece of much-appreciated hoop-iron from his satchel, he wheeled suddenly round, held it to the man's dazzled eyes, and at the same moment wrenched the club from his hand. Chalmers then walked on, feeling considerably relieved, and succeeded in escaping on this occasion.

DANGERS OF THE SURF

everywhere. They have stolen all my beads and hoop-iron. It looks like mischief." Even Chalmers now felt that it was time to retire. "Gould," said he to the mate, "I think we had better get away from here; keep eyes all round, and let us make quietly for the beach." Chalmers used to describe the next quarter of an hour as one of the most uncomfortable in his life. The crowd followed, growling savagely, and one man with a large stone-headed club kept walking just behind the missionary and most unpleasantly near. "Had I that club in my hand," thought Tamate, "I should feel a little more comfortable." A few steps more, and he said to himself: "I *must* have that club, or that club will have me." Wheeling suddenly round, he drew out of his satchel a large piece of hoop-iron, a perfect treasure to a native, and presented it to the savage. The man's eyes glistened as if he had seen a bar of gold, and he stretched out his hand to grasp the prize. In a moment Tamate seized the man's club, wrenched it out of his hand, and brandishing it in the air as if he meant to use it, headed the procession and marched safely down to the boat. Long afterwards, when these natives became his friends, they told him that he "looked bad" at the moment when he took possession of the club; and Chalmers confesses that that was just how he felt.

As we have indicated already, the traveller in New Guinea soon finds that the dangers of the Pacific surf are hardly less than those of the shore or the forest. From the time when as a boy he had learned to swim and row and steer through the often stormy waters of the Highland loch beside which he was born, Tamate had been

AN EXCITING EXPERIENCE

passionately fond of the sea; and it was his constant habit to make trips of exploration along the New Guinea coast in a whale-boat, acting as his own skipper. On the southern coast at certain seasons of the year huge rollers sweep in continually from the Papuan Gulf and burst upon the beach with a noise like thunder. A strong nerve and a cool judgment, as well as a stout arm at the steering-oar, are required if a landing is to be effected in safety; and even to the finest swimmer, to be overturned in the midst of the surf may mean a death either from drowning, or by the teeth of swarming crocodiles, or by being pounded to jelly on the rocks. In the "riding of the surges" Tamate was a master, but though he performed the feat successfully hundreds of times, he once or twice came to grief and had the narrowest escape with his life.

In one of his letters he tells of an exciting experience he had in company with a Mr. Romilly, a Government agent, whom he had taken with him in his whaleboat:—

"We were very deeply laden. On nearing the bar it did not seem to me as *very* dangerous, so we stood on. The first bar sea sped us on, the second one caught us, we shipped water, the steer oar got jammed, the boat swung and went over. It was deep and the seas heavy, and for a short time it seemed some of us must go. It is a terrible place for crocodiles, but I suppose so many of us frightened them. The smashing in the surf was enough to kill. The boat's crew of native students did nobly. We got ashore. I feared at one time Romilly was drowning. I felt somewhat exhausted myself. I fancy Romilly

NEW GUINEA LAKATOIS (SAILING RAFTS MADE OF CANOES LASHED TOGETHER) PREPARING TO SAIL

SERVICES TO BRITISH OFFICIALS

must have been struck with an oar. The boys got the boat in after a good hour's hard work. I got three times on to the boat's keel, and each time was swept away. At last got an oar, and assisted by a native I got to a sandbank—resting a little, then ashore. A fire was lighted, around which we all gathered, when one of the students engaged in prayer, and with full hearts we all joined him in thanksgiving. During the night things were washed ashore, and amongst them my swag."

They spent all that night on the beach, gathered round a fire. Sunday followed. It is not strange to find Chalmers remarking, "We all felt sore and unfit for much exertion." But it is characteristic that he adds that he had two services that day.

The reference which Chalmers makes in the foregoing passage to his having the company of a Government agent on this unlucky trip makes it suitable to mention at this point that in 1884 the British flag was formally hoisted at Port Moresby, and the whole of Southeastern New Guinea declared to be a British Protectorate; while in 1886 this step was followed by the proclamation of Queen Victoria's sovereignty. Of these actions of his Government Chalmers fully approved, and his services to the British officials then and afterwards were of the most valuable kind. No one else knew the country as he did, no one was so familiar with the habits of the people, their languages, and their modes of thought. His work for the Empire has received the most appreciative notice from various quarters. In a letter to the *Times*, written just after the news of Chalmers' death had reached this country, Admiral Bridge says, speaking of the assistance

CHALMERS AS AN EXPLORER

rendered him by Chalmers in 1884-5, "His vigilance, cheeriness, readiness of resource, and extraordinary influence over native savages, made his help quite invaluable. I can honestly say that I do not know how I should have got on without him. He had an equal power of winning the confidence of savages quite unused to strangers, and the respect, and even love, of white seamen. . . . It is difficult to do justice in writing to the character of this really great Englishman. One had only to know and live with him in out-of-the-way lands to be convinced that he was endowed with the splendid characteristics which distinguished our most eminent explorers and pioneers."

Admiral Bridge was right in describing Chalmers as essentially an explorer and pioneer. In many respects he was a man cast in Livingstone's mould, and was never more happy than when pushing his way into regions where the foot of a white man had never trod before. Not only did he explore by whale-boat or steam launch all the coasts and bays of Southern Papua, but he was the first white man to walk right across New Guinea to its eastern end, and he penetrated farther up the difficult Fly River than the most adventurous travellers had ever been before.

And yet he never forgot that his work was primarily that of a Christian teacher, and he never shrank from the little monotonies that were involved. Even when his position became virtually that of a missionary bishop, with duties of superintendence not only over the great Fly River delta, but over the scattered islands of the Torres Straits, he cheerfully undertook day by day the duties of

R. L. STEVENSON AND TAMATE

an elementary schoolmaster. He taught the A B C to young and old—though it should be added that he had the shrewdness to take advantage of the Papuan love of song and music by teaching the people to sing it to the tune of "Auld Lang Syne." One who visited him when he had made his home in the midst of the mangrove swamps of the Fly River found him at daybreak in a rudely constructed schoolhouse which he had built on the sand just above high-water mark. He had a class which was learning English, and with a small bamboo stick for a baton was leading his scholars as they sang, first "God save the Queen," and then "All hail the power of Jesu's name." "I don't think," this friend writes, "that Chalmers ever appeared quite so great a man as when I saw him thus teaching that group of Fly River children."

Thus for five-and-twenty years Tamate of the big warm heart went out and in among the tribes of New Guinea, until his Polynesian name had become a household word alike in the sea-dwellings of the shore, the tree-houses of the hills, and the great *dubus* or barracks in which in the larger communities the people herd together by the hundred. But the day came when Tamate was to go out no more. Writing from Vailima to his mother in November, 1890, Robert Louis Stevenson said of the friend whom he loved and admired so greatly: "I have a *cultus* for Tamate; he is a man nobody can see and not love. . . . . He has plenty of faults like the rest of us; but he's as big as a church." And he expresses the hope that he "shall meet Tamate once more before he

THE LAST EXPEDITION

disappears up the Fly River, perhaps to be one of 'the unreturning brave.'" The words were almost prophetic. Possibly they gave voice to a dim presentiment of which Chalmers himself was sometimes conscious, and of which he may have spoken to his friend.

It was only a few months after, in the beginning of April, 1901, that Tamate set out to visit the district around Cape Blackwood, on the eastern side of the Fly River delta, which was inhabited by a ferocious tribe of savages. He knew that these people were both skull-hunters and cannibals, and for that very reason he had long been eager to get a footing among them. He was accompanied on this occasion by the Rev. Oliver Tomkins, a young and promising colleague lately arrived from England. At a place called Risk Point a swarm of natives, armed with bows and arrows, clubs, knives, and spears, came off in their canoes and took forcible possession of the *Niue*, the little Mission vessel. With the view of inducing them to leave, Tamate decided to go ashore. He did everything he could to persuade Mr. Tomkins to remain on board, probably because he anticipated trouble. Mr. Tomkins, however, refused to allow his leader to go alone; and so the two went off together. Those on board never saw them again, either in life or in death.

The captain of the *Niue* waited for two days, sailing about the coast and keeping a sharp look-out, but no trace could be seen either of the Mission party or their boat. Seeing now that a tragedy must have taken place, he sailed with all speed to Daru and reported the

MURDER OF TAMATE

matter to the British Governor. At once the Governor started in person, accompanied by a sufficient force, in order to find out exactly what had taken place and to inflict punishment if necessary. From a native who was captured he secured the following tale, which was afterwards corroborated in all particulars.

When the two white men got ashore they entered the long *dubu* of the village, their native boys being induced to enter also by the promise of something to eat. No sooner was the whole party within than the signal was given for a general massacre. The first to be killed were the two missionaries, who were knocked simultaneously on the head from behind with stone clubs. Both fell senseless at the first blow, and their heads were immediately cut off. Their followers were then similarly killed and beheaded, though one of them, a powerful man, managed to snatch a club from one of his assailants and kill another at a blow before being himself felled. The heads were distributed as trophies among the murderers. The bodies were cut up and handed over to the women to cook. They were cooked at once, the flesh being mixed with sago, and were eaten the same day.

It was a painful and tragic end to the life of one who, by the testimony of Sir William Macgregor, Governor of New Guinea for seven years, has justly been called "The Apostle of the Papuan Gulf." And yet how much truth there is in the Governor's words in his official report of the massacre and of the steps he felt obliged to take for the punishment of the perpetrators: "I am not alone in the opinion that Mr. Chalmers has won the death he

AUTHORITIES FOR NARRATIVE

would have wished for of all others—in New Guinea and for New Guinea."

The authorities for the life of Chalmers are *Adventures in New Guinea* and *Pioneering in New Guinea*, both by Mr. Chalmers himself; *James Chalmers* and *Tamate*, both by Richard Lovett, M.A. All published by the Religious Tract Society.

CHAPTER X

FATHER DAMIEN OF MOLOKAI

The Hawaiian Islands—Captain Cook and Father Damien—A brave rescue—Molokai and its lepers—Under the pandanus tree—Doctor, undertaker, and grave-digger—What was Father Damien like?—Himself a leper—In life and in death—A statue and a monument.

OF the many archipelagoes scattered over the broad Pacific Ocean none is more intimately associated with names which have gained a lasting and world-wide fame than the Sandwich or, to give them their native name, the Hawaiian Islands. It was on one of this group that Captain Cook, the illustrious navigator, was murdered on February 14th, 1779. It was on another that Father Damien, the humble Belgian priest, "made his great renunciation," as Robert Louis Stevenson called it, "shutting to with his own hand the doors of his own sepulchre" that he might minister to the forsaken lepers of Molokai. No episode of modern missions has thrilled the civilized world more deeply than Father Damien's self-sacrifice. From the Pacific to the Atlantic, by Protestants no less than by Catholics, he has been admiringly crowned as one of the very foremost in the long bead-roll of the martyr-heroes of the Christian faith.

FATHER DAMIEN

He was born in 1840 of peasant parents at a little village on the River Laak, not far from the ancient city of Louvain, in Belgium. His real name was Joseph de Veuster, Damien being a new name which he adopted, according to the custom of the religious orders, when he was admitted to the congregation of the Picpus Fathers. In 1864 he joined on the shortest notice, as a substitute for his elder brother, who had suddenly fallen ill, a band of missionaries for the Hawaiian Islands, and his life's labours were begun in the very island on which Captain Cook met his tragic end so long before. Here for nine years he toiled unsparingly, endearing himself to the natives, and earning from his bishop the title of "the intrepid," because nothing ever seemed to daunt him. He had many adventures both on the sea and among the volcanic mountains, for like Bishop Hannington, whom he frequently recalls, he was a bold cliff-climber and a strong swimmer. In visiting the people in the remoter parts of the island he thought nothing of scaling precipitous rocks on hands and knees, till his boots were torn to shreds and the blood flowed freely from feet as well as hands. Once when his canoe capsized he had to save his life by a long swim in his clothes. On another occasion, as he was riding along a lonely coast, he observed a ship's boat with several persons in it drifting helplessly towards the rocks. Jumping from his horse, he plunged into the sea, and succeeded in reaching the boat and bringing to land eight shipwrecked sailors—three Americans, four Englishmen, and a Dutchman. Their vessel had taken fire in mid-ocean; for more than a week they had drifted about in the Pacific till their strength was utterly exhausted; and

KALAWAO

death was already staring them in the eyes when the brave young priest came with deliverance.

But we must pass from deeds of courage and daring in which Damien has been equalled by many others, to speak of that great deed of sacrifice in which he stands alone. The lovely Hawaiian Islands have long suffered from a terrible scourge, the scourge of leprosy. Some years after Father Damien's arrival the Government determined on the use of drastic measures to stamp out the evil. There is in the archipelago an island called Molokai, which along its northern side presents to the sea an awful front of precipice. At one spot, however, in this frowning battlement of rock, and bearing to it, in R. L. Stevenson's vivid comparison, "the same relation as a bracket to a wall," there projects into the ocean a rugged triangular piece of land known as Kalawao, which is thus "cut off between the surf and the precipice." To this desolate tongue of wind-swept down it was resolved to deport every person, young or old, rich or poor, prince or commoner, in whom the slightest taint of leprosy should be found. The law was carried into effect with the utmost rigour. All over the islands lepers and those suspected of having leprosy were hunted out by the police, dragged away from their homes, and if certified by a doctor as touched by the disease, at once shipped off to the leper settlement as if to a State prison. Children were torn from their parents and parents from their children. Husbands and wives were separated for ever. In no case was any respect of persons shown, and a near relative of the Hawaiian Queen was among the first to be seized and transported.

MOLOKAI AND ITS LEPERS

Awful indeed was the lot of these poor creatures, thus gathered together from all parts of the islands and shot out like rubbish on that dismal wedge of land between cliff and sea. Parted for ever from their friends, outcasts of society, with no man to care for their bodies or their souls, with nothing to hope for but a horrible unpitied death, they gave themselves up to a life like that of the beasts of the field. And even to this day things might have been no better on the peninsula of Kalawao, had it not been for the coming of Father Damien.

For some time Damien had felt the dreadful lot of those unfortunates pressing heavily upon his heart, all the more as several of his own flock had been carried away to the settlement. In a letter written about this time he says that when he saw his own beloved people dragged away, he felt a presentiment that he should see them again. Such a presentiment could only point to one thing. From Molokai no leper was ever permitted to return. Above the beach of Kalawao, as above the arched portal of Dante's Inferno, the awful words might have stood, "Abandon hope all ye who enter here." If Father Damien was to see his poor smitten children again, it must be by going to them, for nevermore should they return to him.

One day there was a gathering of the Roman Catholic clergy at the dedication of a church on the island of Maui, which lies not far from Molokai. After the ceremony was over, the bishop was holding a familiar conversation with his missionaries, and in the course of it he spoke of the distress he felt for the poor lepers of Molokai—stricken

DAMIEN'S PROPOSAL

sheep without a shepherd. At once Damien spoke out. "My lord," he said, "on the day when I was admitted to the order of the Picpus Fathers I was placed under the pall, that I might learn that voluntary death is the beginning of a new life. And I wish to declare now that I am ready to bury myself alive among the lepers of Molokai, some of whom are well known to me."

It shows the stuff of which those Roman Catholic missionaries were made that the bishop accepted Damien's proposal as simply and readily as it was utterd. "I could not have imposed this task upon any one," he said; "but I gladly accept the offer you have made." At once Damien was ready to start, for, like General Gordon when he started for Khartoum, he required no time for preparations. A few days afterwards, on May 11th, 1873, he was landed on the beach of Kalawao along with a batch of fifty miserable lepers, whom the authorities had just collected from various parts of Hawaii.

The sights that met the eye of the devoted missionary must have been revolting beyond expression, though Damien himself says little about them, for it was not his habit to dwell on these details. Stevenson visited Molokai after Damien was dead, and after the place had been "purged, bettered, beautified" by his influence and example; but he describes the experience as "grinding" and "harrowing." The Princess-Regent of Hawaii once paid a State visit to the settlement while Damien was there, and after his presence had wrought a marvellous transformation. The lepers were dressed in their best. Triumphal arches adorned the beach. Flowers were strewn in profusion along the path that led to the place

UNDER THE PANDANUS TREE

of reception. But when the royal lady looked around her on that awful crowd, the tears rolled down her cheeks, and though it had been arranged that she should speak to the people, her lips trembled so helplessly that she was unable to utter a single word. Damien came to Kalawao when the settlement was at its worst. He saw it too, not as a passing visitor, but as one who knew that henceforth this was to be his only home on earth. He confesses that for a moment, as he stepped ashore, his heart sank within him. But he said to himself, "Now, Joseph, my boy, this is your life-work!" And never during the sixteen years that followed did he go back upon his resolve.

For several weeks, until he found time to build himself a hut, he had no shelter but a large pandanus tree. This pandanus tree he called his house, and under its branches he lay down on the ground to sleep at night. Meanwhile, from the very first, he spent his days in trying to teach and help and comfort his leper flock. In a letter to his brother, Father Pamphile, in substitution for whom, as mentioned already, he had become a Hawaiian missionary, he admits that at first he almost grew sick in the presence of so much physical corruption. On Sundays especially, when the people crowded closely round him in the little building which served as a chapel, he often felt as if he must rush out of the loathsome atmosphere into the open air. But he deliberately crushed these sensations down. He sought to make himself as one of the lepers, and carried this so far that in his preaching he did not use the conventional "My brethren," but employed the expression "We

DOCTOR, UNDERTAKER, Etc.

lepers" instead. And by and by the spirit of sympathy grew so strong that even in the presence of what was most disgusting all feeling of repugnance passed entirely away.

It was not only the souls of the lepers for which Father Damien cared. At that time there was no doctor in the settlement, so he set himself to soothe their bodily sufferings as best he could, cleansing their open wounds and binding up their stumps and sores. Death was constantly busy—indeed, some one died almost every day; and whether at noon or at midnight, the good father was there to perform the last offices of his Church. And as he sought to comfort the lepers in dying, his care for them continued after they were dead. Before his arrival no one had thought of burying a dead leper with any sort of decency. No coffin was provided; the corpse at best was shovelled hastily into a shallow hole. But Father Damien's reverence for a human being forbade him to acquiesce in such arrangements. As there was no one else to make coffins he made them himself, and it is estimated that during his years on Molokai he made not less than 1500 with his own hands. More than this. When no other could be got to dig a proper grave, Damien did not hesitate to seize his spade and act the part of the grave-digger. To most people such toils as pastor and preacher, doctor and undertaker, would seem more than enough even for the strongest of men. But they were far from summing up the labours of Damien. He induced the people to build themselves houses, and as few of them knew how to begin, he became head-mason and carpenter-in-chief to the whole settlement. He next got them to give him their assist-

WHAT WAS DAMIEN LIKE?

ance in erecting suitable chapels at different points of the peninsula. He built two orphanages, one for boys and one for girls, into which he gathered all the fatherless and motherless children; and to the instruction of these young people he gave special attention. Above all, he sought by constant cheerfulness and unflagging energy to infuse a new spirit into that forlorn collection of doomed men and women. By teaching them to work he brought a fresh and healthy interest into their lives. By creating a Christian public opinion he lifted them out of the condition of filth and sottishness into which they had sunk. But, above all, he wiped off from their souls "the soiling of despair" by the assurance he gave them of human sympathy and Divine love.

What was Father Damien like? many will ask. He was tall and strong, indeed of an imposing presence, with a bright and serene countenance and a rich and powerful voice. The very sight of him brought strength and comfort to others. Like the Master Whom he loved and sought to follow, and Who also was the Friend of the leper, he was possessed of a strange magnetism—a kind of vital "virtue"—which, though in Damien's case it could not effect miracles, yet had power to lift up the hearts of those who were bowed down by their infirmities.

So the years passed on, while day after day was filled up with such tasks as we have described. During the first six months the father was sometimes haunted by the thought that he had contracted the insidious disease, but thereafter he banished the idea from his mind, and lived on in Molokai for many years in perfect health and

HIMSELF A LEPER

strength. One day, however, as he was washing his feet in unusually hot water, he noticed that they had been blistered with the heat without his being conscious of any pain. At once he knew what this meant. He had not lived so long in the settlement without learning that the absence of feeling in any part of the body is one of the surest symptoms of leprosy; and now he understood that his doom was sealed. But the fact made very little difference in either his thoughts or his ways. So long as he was able he went on with his duties as before, while he exerted himself with special anxiety to secure that after he was gone the work he had been doing in the settlement should be carried on, and carried on still more efficiently than had been possible for one who laboured single-handed. And before he died he had the joy of knowing not only that these deeds of love and mercy would be taken up and continued by other fathers of his order, but that a band of Franciscan sisters, inspired by his great example, had volunteered to serve as nurses among the lepers of Molokai, and that an adequate hospital with a thoroughly qualified doctor would seek to assuage the sufferings of those who had reached the last stages of the fatal malady.

In spite of all that Father Damien accomplished when he was alive, we might almost say that he did more for the Hawaiian lepers by his death than by his life. It was not till after he had passed away that men came to a full knowledge of this hero of the nineteenth century. Largely by the help of the burning pen of Robert Louis Stevenson, the story of his willing martyrdom flew round the world and made the name of Molokai illustrious. International

A STATUE AND A MONUMENT

sympathy was aroused for the poor sufferers for whom Damien laid down his life. The Press of every Christian country resounded with his fame. Princes and peasants sought to do him honour. His Royal Highness the Prince of Wales—now King Edward VII—placed himself at the head of a movement which had for its object to commemorate the life and labours of this brave soldier-saint of Jesus Christ. Money flowed in, by which it became possible to do much more for Damien's leper flock than he had ever been able to do himself. The Damien Institute was formed in England for the training of Roman Catholic youths to the laborious life of missionary priests in the South Seas.

When Father Damien's end was drawing near, he expressed a desire to be buried at the foot of the pandanus tree beneath which he had lived when he first came to Molokai. The two fathers who were now with him thought it right to comply with his wishes; and so under the very spot which once served him for his bed his body lies awaiting the Resurrection, with flowers growing over it and the wide tree spreading above. In one of the streets of Louvain there stands a beautiful statue of Father Damien. His face is uplifted to heaven, his left hand holds a crucifix to his heart, his right arm is thrown in love and protection round the shoulder of a poor leper, who crouches to his side for comfort. It is a fine conception, finely executed; and yet its effect upon the beholder can hardly compare with the feelings of those who, like Stevenson and other pilgrims to the island, have stood by that grave in Molokai beneath the old pandanus tree and seen Father Damien's monument lying

AN ACKNOWLEDGMENT

all around him in that community of lepers, which has been "purged, bettered, beautified" by his great act of sacrifice.

The author desires to acknowledge his obligation to Father Pamphile de Veuster's translation of *Father Damien: Apostle of the Lepers of Molokai*, by the Rev. Philibert Tauvel, ss.cc. The book is published for the Picpus Fathers of the Damien Institute, Eccleshall, Staffordshire, by the Art and Book Company, London. R. L. Stevenson's *Father Damien* is, of course, invaluable as a sidelight to the biography.

CHAPTER XI

AMONG THE CANNIBAL ISLANDS

The Fiji Islands—Man-eating—Human sacrifice—King George of Tonga—James Calvert—The King of Bau—The man-hunters—Two brave ladies—Murder of widows—King Thakombau and Queen Victoria—A happy Christian warrior.

ALMOST due north of New Zealand, but at a distance of nearly 1200 miles, there lies embosomed in the midst of the Pacific Ocean a British group of islands of surpassing loveliness—one of the fairest jewel clusters in King Edward's crown. They are about two hundred and fifty in number, ranging from the size of a large English county to barren rocks which disappear altogether at the highest tides. To the invariable beauty of all volcanic islands in the tropics this group adds the peculiar charms of the coral formations of the Pacific. Mountains clothed in the most luxuriant vegetation toss their fretted peaks high into the air. Great green breakers dash perpetually on the barrier reefs, sending their snowy foam up to the very roots of the cocoanut trees that fringe the long shining beaches. Inside of the reefs, again, the lagoon lies sleeping, indigo-blue where its waters are deepest, emerald-green nearer to the shore; but always of such crystal clearness that the idle occupant of a canoe can see far down at the bottom the white sands,

THE FIJI ISLANDS

the richly tinted seaweeds, the exquisite coral growths—branching into innumerable varieties of form, and blossoming with all the colours of the rainbow. These are the Fiji Islands, ceded by King Thakombau to Queen Victoria in 1874. King Edward is now the real King of Fiji. But if it had not been for the splendid labours of a band of Wesleyan missionaries, of whom the Rev. James Calvert was the most notable, the possession of Fiji would have brought the British monarch the questionable honour of being a "King of the Cannibal Islands."

It was not of Fiji that Bishop Heber wrote,

> Though every prospect pleases,
> And only man is vile.

But to these islands some sixty years ago the words might very fitly have been applied. Even among the savage peoples of the South Seas the Fijians were notorious for every kind of brutal abomination. Man-eating was not only practised, but gloried in and gloated over. It had become a lust so overmastering that men were known to murder their nearest relatives in order to gratify the craving for human flesh. To such an extent was it carried on that there were some who could boast of having eaten hundreds of their fellow-creatures. Miss Gordon Cumming, in her most interesting book, *At Home in Fiji*, tells of a row of stones she saw, extending to a distance of 200 yards, which was nothing else than a cannibal register formerly kept by two chiefs to represent the number of persons they had themselves eaten—each stone standing for a human body. Woe betide the unfortunate crew whose ship drifted on to the reefs of a Fiji island! If they

HUMAN SACRIFICES

escaped from the cruel breakers, it was only to be dispatched by a club as soon as they reached the shore, and cooked forthwith in a huge cannibal oven.

But cannibalism was only one of the many forms of Fijian cruelty. In these fair islands, one might say, the air was always tainted with the smell of blood, for without the sacrifice of human blood nothing of importance could be undertaken. If a war canoe was to be launched, it was dragged down to the water over the prostrate bodies of living men and women, who were always mangled, and often crushed to death in the process. When a chief's house was being built, deep holes were dug for the wooden pillars on which the house was to rest. A man was thrown into each hole, and he was compelled to stand clasping the pillar with his arms while the earth was filled in right over his head. At the death of a Fijian of any consequence all his wives were strangled and buried beside him to furnish what was called "lining for his grave." His mother also, if still alive, suffered the same fate; and it was the duty of the eldest son to take the leading part in the strangling of both his mother and grandmother. The lives of more distant female relatives and connexions were spared, but they had to express their grief by sawing off one of their fingers with a sharp shell, joint by joint, so that it was hardly possible to see a woman in the islands who had not suffered mutilation in both her hands.

In spite of their cruelty, however, the Fijians were a race much superior, both in physique and intelligence, to the majority of the South Sea islanders. Usually tall and muscular, both men and women sometimes displayed pro-

KING GEORGE OF TONGA

portions that were quite magnificent. Their social laws were elaborate, and they possessed some of the arts of civilization. As manufacturers of cloth, and especially of pottery, they were famous far and wide in the Pacific, and canoes came hundreds of miles from other island groups to purchase their ware. They also enjoyed a unique reputation as wig-makers and hairdressers. Every chief had his own private hair artist, who spent hours each day over his master's head. With all kinds of fantastic variations in the particular style, the general idea was to get the hair to stick out as far as possible from the skull; and specially skilful operators were able to produce a coiffure five feet in circumference. Like everything else in this world, however, this elaborate top-dressing had to be paid for, and the payment came at bedtime. It was impossible to lay such a head upon a pillow, much more upon the ground. The Fijian had to rest his neck all night long on a bar of bamboo raised above the floor by two short legs.

It was between the thirties and the forties that the first pioneers of Christianity came to Fiji. About 250 miles to the east lie the Friendly Islands, inhabited by a race called Tongans. These Tongans were much bolder sailors than most of the South Sea races, and were in the habit of visiting Fiji periodically for purposes of trade. Eventually some of them settled in the most easterly islands of the group, a fact which led to still closer intercourse. In the Friendly Islands the Wesleyan missionaries had met with remarkable success. The Tongans nearly all became Christians, including their king, King George, as he was called after his baptism. In

JAMES CALVERT

his heathen days this man had been a famous fighter, leading out his war canoes, like some Viking of the Pacific, and spreading death and devastation far and near. Now that he was a Christian he was no less zealous in seeking to spread the Gospel of peace. Both he and his people were especially anxious that Christianity should be carried to Fiji, and they persuaded the Wesleyans to make the attempt. The Rev. James Calvert was among the pioneers in this dangerous enterprise; the only one who was spared to see the marvellous transformation which passed over the archipelago within the course of a single generation, and can only be compared to the transition that takes place within a single hour in those same tropical regions from the darkness of the night to the glory of the morning.

It was in Lakemba, one of the eastern or windward islands, as they are called, that Mr. and Mrs. Calvert first landed. It was a suitable place in which to begin, for here they were in the neighbourhood of the Tongan colonies where King George's influence was felt. All the same, they were subjected to a great deal of unkindness, and had to face constant dangers and hardships, especially as Mr. Calvert's district covered not Lakemba only, but twenty-four surrounding islands. Many days and nights had to be spent on the ocean in frail canoes. Many an anxious hour Mrs. Calvert had in Lakemba, alone in the midst of fierce savages, thinking, too, of her absent husband, who might be battling with the storm in a sea full of coral reefs, or standing unarmed in the midst of a throng of excited cannibals.

After some years of labour in their first sphere, it was

THE KING OF BAU

decided that the Calverts should leave the eastern outskirts of the archipelago and make for the very citadel of Fijian heathenism and savagery. In the island of Bau, which lies near the heart of the whole group, there lived at that time an old king called Tanoa, one of the most ferocious of man-eaters, and his son Thakombau, a prince of almost gigantic size and at the same time of unusual intelligence and character. Both the king of Bau and his son were celebrated warriors. In case of need they could summon to their banner many scores of war canoes, and their power to strike was felt all over Fiji. Thakombau was capable of mildness, but with Tanoa blood-thirstiness had become a kind of mania. When he went forth in his huge sailing canoe to demand tribute from surrounding islands, nothing delighted him so much as to exact little children and to sail back to harbour with their bodies dangling from his yard-arms. Once a near kinsman had offended him, and though the culprit begged his pardon most humbly, Tanoa only responded by cutting off the arm of the poor wretch at the elbow and drinking the warm blood as it flowed. Next he cooked the arm and ate it in the presence of his victim, and finally had him cut to pieces limb by limb. He was no more merciful to his own children than to those of other people, and on one occasion compelled one of his sons to club a younger brother to death.

With characteristic courage the Wesleyan missionaries determined to strike at the very centre of Fijian cruelty, for they knew that if heathenism could be cast down in Bau, the effects of its downfall would be felt in every island of the archipelago. On Bau itself Tanoa would by

THE MAN-HUNTERS

no means permit them to settle, nor would he allow any Christian services to be held in that island. He made no objections, however, to Mr. Calvert's building a house on an islet called Viwa, which is separated from Bau by only two miles of water, and he was quite willing to receive personal visits. Mr. Calvert had many a conversation with the old king and his son. On Tanoa he made not the slightest impression; but over Thakombau he gradually gained an influence which was to lead in due course both to the Christianization of the Fiji Islands and to their incorporation in Britain's world-wide empire.

But it was Mrs. Calvert, not her husband, who gained the first victory in the fight. Hospitality was a thing on which King Tanoa prided himself, and he never failed to entertain important guests with a banquet of human flesh. If enemies could be secured for the table, so much the better; but if not, he had no hesitation in sacrificing his own subjects. On one occasion a party of envoys from a piratical tribe had come to Bau to offer the king a share of their spoil by way of tribute. At once a hunting-party was sent out under the leadership of Ngavindi, a notable chief, which soon returned with fourteen captures, all women—woman being considered an even greater delicacy than man. In those days the fishing in Fiji was nearly all done by the gentler sex, and these unfortunates were wading in the sea with their nets when the hunters sighted them. Creeping up with his men under the cover of a fringe of mangrove bushes which ran along the shore, Ngavindi dashed suddenly into the water and seized the screaming women, who knew only too well what sort of fate awaited them. Word of the occurrence

TWO BRAVE LADIES

came to Viwa almost immediately. Mr. Calvert was absent at the time on one of his numerous expeditions, but his wife and another lady who was with her resolved to do what they could to save the doomed wretches. They jumped into a canoe and paddled hastily across the strait. Before they reached the shore the din of the death-drums told them that the work of butchery had already begun. Every moment was precious now, and when they got to land they took to their heels and ran towards the king's house. By the laws of Bau no woman was at liberty to cross Tanoa's threshold on pain of her life, unless he sent for her; but these two ladies thought nothing of their own danger. They rushed headlong into the king's presence, and with arms outstretched besought him to spare the remaining victims. The very boldness of their action made it successful. Tanoa seemed quite dumbfounded by their audacity, but he at once ordered the work of slaughter to cease. Nine of the poor women had already been killed and carried off to the ovens, but the remaining five were immediately set at liberty.

There was another custom not less cruel than cannibalism, and even more difficult to uproot, since it was deeply intertwined with the religious ideas of the people and especially with their thoughts about the future life. This was the practice already referred to of strangling a man's wives and even his mother on the occasion of his funeral, so that their spirits might accompany him into the invisible world. As King Tanoa was an old man whose end seemed to be drawing near, the prospect of his death and what might happen in connexion with it gave Mr. Calvert the deepest concern. He knew that if Fijian usage was

MURDER OF WIDOWS

adhered to, the departure of so great a chieftain from the world was sure to be attended by a wholesale immolation of his women-folk. He also saw that if the practice could be broken down at Tanoa's obsequies, a deadly blow would be struck at such abominations. He therefore visited Thakombau, the heir-apparent, again and again, and urged him by every consideration in his power to abandon the idea of slaughtering his father's wives. He tried to appeal to his better feelings; he promised to give him a very handsome present if he would refrain from blood; he even went so far as to offer to cut off his own finger, after the Fijian fashion of mourning, if the women might be spared. But though Thakombau was evidently impressed by Mr. Calvert's pleadings, he would give no assurance, and Mr. Calvert learned afterwards that all the while Tanoa himself had been privately instructing his son that his wives must on no account be kept from accompanying him on his journey into the unseen.

The old king's death took place rather suddenly in the end, and on this occasion too Mr. Calvert happened to be absent on duty in a distant island, so that it fell to a younger missionary, Mr. Watsford, to take action. As soon as he heard of the death, he made for Bau with all possible haste. Within Tanoa's house and in the very presence of the corpse the work of massacre had begun. Two wives were lying dead, and a third had been summoned, when the missionary burst in. When Thakombau saw him enter he became greatly excited, and trembling from head to foot he cried out, "What about it, Mr. Watsford?" "Refrain, sir!" Mr. Watsford exclaimed, speaking with great difficulty, for his emotions almost

KING THAKOMBAU

overpowered him. "Refrain! that is plenty; two are dead.' But though Thakombau was moved, he would not yield. "They are not many," he said, "only five. But for you missionaries, many more would have accompanied my father." And so the other three victims were brought in —newly bathed, anointed with oil, dressed in their best as if going to a joyous feast. And there, in the very presence of the white man as he kept pleading for their lives, they were put to death in the usual way. They were made to kneel down on the floor; a cord was fastened round their necks; and this cord was gradually drawn tighter and tighter till life was extinct.

But though King Thakombau had not the courage at this time to defy the ancient traditions of his people, the influence of a higher teaching had been slowly telling upon him, and the day-dawn in Fiji was about to begin. Soon after Tanoa's funeral a Bau chief died, and Mr. Calvert was able in this case to persuade Thakombau to forbid any sacrifice of the women of the house. The usual preparations for murder had already been made, and the royal command gave great offence to many. The chief executioner flung down his strangling-cord and exclaimed, "Then I suppose we are to die like anybody now!" But a great victory had been won for humanity and Christianity. A precedent against a brutal custom had been established, which made it much easier for all time coming to rescue the proposed victims of superstition and cruelty.

But the greatest triumph of all came when Thakombau resolved to renounce heathenism altogether and take his stand on the Christian side. In the presence of a vast

PRESENTS TO QUEEN VICTORIA

crowd, summoned by the beating of the very death-drums which had formerly rolled out their invitation to the islanders to be present at a cannibal feast, the king of Bau renounced his past, proclaimed his faith, and declared his intention to live henceforth as a follower of Christ. That day of 1857 was not only a day of gratitude and thanksgiving in the experience of Mr. Calvert and his colleagues, but one of the most important days in the history of Fiji. It was the precursor, indeed, of another day some seventeen years later when Thakombau, having applied to be taken under the protection of the British Crown, formally ceded the Fiji Islands to Queen Victoria, handing over at the same time to the British Envoy his old war-club, in token of the fact that his people were now "abandoning club law and adopting the forms and principles of civilized society." Thakombau's magnificent club, together with his drinking-bowl, of which he made a present to our Queen, may now be seen by interested visitors in the British Museum. Innocent as they now look in their Museum case, it requires some exercise of the imagination to picture forth the awful scenes of massacre and the loathsome cannibal orgies in which that same club and drinking-bowl once had their share.

This book is called *The Romance of Missionary Heroism.* To those who read his story afterwards, the heroism and romance of a missionary's life often lies in the faith and courage and tenacity with which he faced toils and dangers, even though his endeavours did not result in great outward achievements. But there are other cases in which the romance of the missionary adventurer's life appears not only in the trials and difficulties he faces, but in the

A HAPPY CHRISTIAN WARRIOR

wonderful victories he wins. Now and then there comes a fortunate knight of Christ before whom embattled hosts go down, and who wins his way into the City of Jerusalem and claims it in his Lord's name. James Calvert was such a happy knight. When he and his young wife reached Fiji, one of his first tasks was to gather up and bury the skulls, hands, and feet of eighty men and women who had been sacrificed at a single feast. All around them day by day deeds of horror went on which might well have frozen the blood of any one who was not sustained by faith in God. Men and women bound with ropes were dragged past their door, going literally like oxen to the slaughter. The very air they breathed was foul at times with the sickening odour of roasting human flesh. Yet they hardly dared to express their disgust and loathing. A brother missionary and his wife narrowly escaped from being themselves burnt alive because the lady had ventured to close the window and draw down the blind in order to shut out the sight and smell of what was going on in front of their house. On his visits to strange islands, too, Mr. Calvert always went with his life in his hand, and more than once had marvellous escapes from a death that seemed certain. But this same missionary, who had seen Fiji in its midnight gloom, was spared to see it in the light of the sun-rising. He was spared to see the islands provided with 1300 Christian churches, crowded Sunday after Sunday by devout congregations. And where once the stillness of the night had been often broken by the death-shriek of the victim or the cannibal's exultant death-song, he was spared to hear, as he passed along the village paths

SOURCES OF THE NARRATIVE

after dark had fallen, the voices of fathers, mothers, and little children rising together from many a home in sweet evening hymns.

LITERATURE.—*Cannibals and Saints*, by James Calvert; *At Home in Fiji*, by Miss C. F. Gordon Cumming (William Blackwood and Sons); *James Calvert*, by R. Vernon (S. W. Partridge and Co.).

CHAPTER XII

THE APOSTLE OF THE NEW HEBRIDES

John Williams and John G. Paton—First night on Tanna—A lonely grave—The power of an empty revolver—Savages foiled by a retriever—A tragedy on Erromanga—The sandal-wood traders—H.M.S. *Pelorus*—Bishop Selwyn's testimony—The power of prayer—"The last awful night"—Facing the cannibals—Jehovah's rain—Epilogue.

OF all the many island clusters of the South Pacific there is none, perhaps, which has so good a claim as the New Hebrides to be regarded as classic ground in the history of Christian missions. It was on Erromanga, one of this group, that John Williams, the greatest of all the missionaries of Oceania, the "Apostle of the South Seas," as he has justly been called, fell in death under the club of a fierce cannibal. And it was on Tanna, an adjacent island, that the veteran Dr. John G. Paton, a man not less apostolic than John Williams, began a career so full of intrepid action and hairbreadth escape, of thrilling adventure and extraordinary romance, mingled at times with dreadful tragedy, that more almost than any other in the missionary annals of modern times it serves to illustrate the saying, "Truth is stranger than fiction."

FIRST NIGHT ON TANNA

It is nearly fifty years since Dr. Paton was sent out by the Reformed Presbyterian Church of Scotland to begin his life-work among the cannibals of the New Hebrides. Tanna was the island chosen for his sphere, an island hitherto untouched by Christianity; and the Tannese were among the most ferocious savages of those southern seas.

When he landed, war was afoot between an inland tribe and a tribe of the shore. He tells how, on the very first night that he spent on Tanna, five or six men who had been killed in the fighting were cooked and eaten at a neighbouring spring, so that next morning, when he wanted some water to make tea for his breakfast, the spring was so polluted with blood that it could not be used. On the second evening the quiet of the night was broken by a sound more blood-curdling even than the howls of infuriated warriors—" a wild, wailing cry from the villages around, long-continued and unearthly." It told of the strangling of the widow, that she might accompany her dead husband into the other world and be his servant there as she had been here

At first Mr. Paton had the companionship of his brave young wife amidst the trials and perils which had daily to be faced. But in a few months she was cut off by fever, together with the little son who had just been born to them. The lonely man had to dig a grave with his own hands, and lay the bodies of his beloved ones in the dust. At this time, when he was almost distracted with grief, a providential visit from Bishop Selwyn and Mr. Coleridge Patteson in their Mission ship brought him the consolation of true Christian sympathy. "Standing with me," he

A LONELY GRAVE

writes, "beside the grave of mother and child, I weeping aloud on his one hand, and Patteson—afterwards the Martyr Bishop of Nukapu—sobbing silently on the other, the godly Bishop Selwyn poured out his heart to God amidst sobs and tears, during which he laid his hands on my head, and invoked Heaven's richest consolations and blessings on me and my trying labours."

Strengthened by this angel visit from the noble pair of Church of England missionaries, Mr. Paton set to work once more, though day by day he was made to feel that his life hung by a single thread. Constantly the savages threatened him with death; sometimes during the night they made cowardly attempts upon his life. But in some way or other—the stumbling of an assailant, the barking of his trusty dog, the working of superstitious fear in a heathen heart—the danger was always turned aside.

One morning before daybreak Mr. Paton was wakened by the noise of shots being fired along the beach. He had brought a few native teachers from the Christian island of Aneityum to help him in his work, and one of these men rushed in breathlessly to say that six or seven natives had been shot dead to make provision for a great cannibal feast, and that the murderers were coming to kill Mr. Paton and the Aneityumese for the same purpose.

At once he called all the teachers into the house, locked the door, and barred the window. By and by the tramp of many approaching feet was heard. And all through the morning and the long forenoon the cannibals kept running round the house, whispering to one another, and hovering about the window and the door. But the

POWER OF AN EMPTY REVOLVER

expected attack was never made. The Tannese knew that Mr. Paton had a fowling-piece and a revolver in the house; they did not know that he had vowed never to use them to destroy human lives. And the fear of these weapons in a white man's hands must have held them back, for towards noon they stole silently away, and held their gruesome feast without the addition of Christian victims.

Amidst scenes like this Mr. Paton went on steadily with his work, teaching all whom he could get to listen, mastering the language, translating parts of the Bible into Tannese, and printing them with a little printing-press that he had got from Scotland. He was greatly cheered at last by the arrival of another missionary, Mr. Johnston, who was accompanied by his wife. But not long after their arrival a painful tragedy befell.

It was New Year's night, and the Johnstons had joined Mr. Paton at family worship. Worship over, they retired to their own cabin, which was only a few yards off; but Mr. Johnston came back immediately to inform Mr. Paton that two men with painted faces were standing just outside his window armed with huge clubs.

Going out, Mr. Paton at once confronted these nocturnal visitors, and asked them what they wanted. "Medicine for a sick boy," they replied. He told them to come in and get it, but the agitation they showed, and their evident unwillingness to come into the light of the room, made him suspect that they had some murderous design. He allowed no sign of his thoughts to appear, however, but stepped, along with Mr. Johnston, into the house, followed by the two men; and, keeping a watchful eye on them all the while, quietly prepared the medicine.

DR. PATON'S LIFE SAVED BY HIS FAITHFUL DOGS

FOILED BY A RETRIEVER

When he came forward with it the men, instead of taking it, tightened their grasp upon their killing-stones. But his steady gaze seemed to cow them, and when he sternly ordered them to leave the house they turned away.

At that moment Mr. Johnston stooped down to lift a little kitten of Mr. Paton's that was running out at the door, and instantly one of the savages leaped forward and aimed a blow at the stooping man. Mr. Johnston saw it coming, and in trying to avoid it rolled over and fell prostrate on the floor.

Quick as thought, Mr. Paton sprang in between his friend and the savages, upon which the two men turned on him and raised their stone clubs in the air to strike him down. He was saved by the courage and fidelity of his two dogs. One of them in particular, a little cross-bred retriever with terrier's blood in him, showed the utmost boldness, and sprang furiously at the faces of the cannibals. The dog was badly hurt, but the savages were foiled, and at last they took to their heels through the door.

Accustomed to such scenes, Mr. Paton retired to rest, and slept soundly. With the newly arrived missionary it was otherwise. He had received a nervous shock, from which he never recovered; and in three weeks he was dead. Again Mr. Paton had to make a coffin and dig a grave. And then, he says, referring to the heart-broken young widow and himself, " We two alone at sunset laid him to rest close by the Mission House, beside my own dear wife and child."

Shortly after this a dreadful deed of blood was wrought

A TRAGEDY ON ERROMANGA

on Erromanga, where John Williams had been murdered fully twenty years before. The Rev. Mr. Gordon and his wife, Presbyterian missionaries from Nova Scotia, had been settled on the island, and were making some inroads on its heathendom. But the sandalwood traders of the New Hebrides, a very debased set of men in those days, hated Mr. Gordon because he denounced their atrocities and warned the natives against their vices. In revenge they excited the superstitions of the Erromangans by persuading them that a plague of measles and a hurricane, both of which had recently visited the island, were brought about by Mr. Gordon. Thus the sandalwooders were responsible for a calamity which made Erromanga once more a martyr isle, and all but led to a scene of martyrdom on Tanna also.

One day, when Mr. Gordon was hard at work thatching a printing shed, in which he hoped to provide the Erromangans with the Word of God in their own tongue, two men came to him and begged for medicine. At once he left his work and started with them towards the Mission House. As he was stepping over a streamlet that ran across the path his foot slipped, and that moment the two men were upon him with their tomahawks. A terrible blow on the spine laid him on the ground; a second on the neck almost parted his head from his body. Immediately a band of natives, who had been hiding in the surrounding bush, rushed out and danced in frantic joy round the dead missionary.

Meanwhile Mrs. Gordon, hearing the noise, came out of the house, wondering what had happened. The spot where her murdered husband lay was fortunately concealed

MR. PATON THREATENED

from her eyes by a clump of trees. One of the natives approached her, and when she asked him what the noise meant, told her that it was only the boys amusing themselves. Then, as she turned to gaze once more in the direction of the shouting, he crept stealthily behind her, drove his tomahawk into her back, and severed her neck with his next blow.

Just after this double murder a sandalwood trader brought a party of Erromangans over to Tanna in his boat. These Erromangans urged the Tannese to kill Mr. Paton as they themselves had killed the Gordons; and though some of the Tanna chiefs refused to have anything to do with the business, the great majority of them began to cry aloud for the missionary's death. Crowds came flocking to the Mission House and shouting in Mr. Paton's hearing, "The men of Erromanga killed Missi Williams long ago, and now they have killed Missi Gordon. Let us kill Missi Paton too, and drive the worship of Jehovah from our land." Another favourite cry of the time, and one that boded ill for this "much-enduring" man, whose constant perils, adventures, and escapes recall the story of old Ulysses—was "Our love to the Erromangans! Our love to the Erromangans!"

At this juncture, just when Mr. Paton's life from day to day seemed to be hanging by a single hair, two British warships sailed into the harbour. Seeing the state of matters, the Commodore urged Mr. Paton to leave Tanna at once, and offered to convey him either to New Zealand, or to the island of Aneityum, where Christianity had obtained a firm footing. But though grateful for the Commodore's kindness, he firmly declined

H.M.S. "PELORUS"

to leave his post. He knew that if he did so his station would immediately be broken up, and all the labours of the past three or four years would go for nothing. Moreover, in spite of all that had happened, in spite of the fact that so many of the people would willingly have put him to death, he loved those cruel savages with that Christian love which sees the latent possibilities of goodness in the very worst of men. To him a troop of howling cannibals, literally thirsting for his blood, were his "dear benighted Tannese" after all.

It takes a hero to understand a hero. And it may help us to appreciate Mr. Paton's heroism in standing fast at what he felt to be the post of duty, when we find what Bishop Selwyn thought of it after hearing the whole story of the incident from Commodore Seymour's own lips. Describing to a friend how the brave Scotchman had declined to leave Tanna by H.M.S. *Pelorus*, he added, "And I like him all the better for so doing." The following words in one of his letters show how high he rated Mr. Paton's conduct:—

"Talk of bravery! talk of heroism! The man who leads a forlorn hope is a coward in comparison with him, who, on Tanna, thus alone, without a sustaining look or cheering word from one of his own race, regards it as his duty to hold on in the face of such dangers. We read of the soldier, found after the lapse of ages among the ruins of Herculaneum, who stood firm at his post amid the fiery rain destroying all around him, thus manifesting the rigidity of the discipline amongst those armies of ancient Rome which conquered the world. Mr. Paton was subjected to no such iron law. He might, with honour,

ATTACKED IN THE BUSH

when offered to him, have sought a temporary asylum in Auckland, where he would have been heartily received. But he was moved by higher considerations. He chose to remain, and God knows whether at this moment he is in the land of the living."

After the departure of the men-of-war, constant attempts were made on Mr. Paton's life. Sometimes his empty revolver drove away his cowardly assailants. Frequently he was delivered by his perfect faith in the Divine protection and the confidence with which he asserted that faith. Once, for example, as he was going along a path in the bush, a man sprang suddenly from behind a bread-fruit tree, and swinging his tomahawk on high with a fiendish look, aimed it straight for Mr. Paton's brow. Springing aside, the missionary avoided the blow. And before the ruffian could raise his weapon a second time, he turned upon him and said in a voice in which there was no fear, "If you dare to strike me, my Jehovah God will punish you. He is here to defend me now." At once the man trembled from head to foot, and looked all round to see if this Jehovah God might not be standing near among the shadows.

Another time it seemed that the end had surely come. A conch shell was heard pealing out a warlike summons. Evidently it was a preconcerted signal, for the ominous notes had not died away before there was seen an immense multitude of armed savages advancing at the double down the slopes of a hill some distance off. Abandoning the Mission House, Mr. Paton with his native teachers escaped through the bush to the village of a half-friendly chief some miles away; but it was not long till the savages were hot-foot on their trail.

THE POWER OF PRAYER

The fugitives saw them coming, and knew that God alone could save them. "We prayed," says Dr. Paton, "as one can only pray when in the jaws of death." And then a strange thing happened. When about 300 yards off, the pursuers suddenly stood stock-still. The chief with whom he had taken refuge touched Mr. Paton's knee and said, "Missi, Jehovah is hearing!" And to this day Dr. Paton can give no other explanation of what took place. That host of warriors, to whom no opposition could possibly have been offered, hesitated, turned back, and disappeared into the forest.

At length there came what Dr. Paton's brother and editor describes as "the last awful night." Driven from his own station, Mr. Paton had succeeded, after encountering dreadful risks and hardships by sea and land, in joining Mr. and Mrs. Mathieson, who occupied another post of the Mission at the opposite end of Tanna. But soon the cannibals were on his track again, and the crisis came which led to the breaking up for a time of all Christian work on Tanna.

The Mission House was in a state of siege, and Mr. Paton, worn out with fatigue and constant watching, had fallen into a deep sleep. He was wakened by his faithful dog Clutha pulling at his clothes. Feeling sure that the instincts of the animal had not deceived it, and that even in the dead silence of the night it must have scented some danger, Mr. Paton wakened his companions.

Hardly had he done so when a glare of red light fell into the room. Then dark figures were seen flitting to and fro with blazing torches and making for the adjoining church, which was speedily in flames. Next the sav-

"YOU MUST KILL ME FIRST"

These were the brave words of a chief who, when many of the natives were intent on killing Dr. Paton, sided with him and saved his life.

FACING THE CANNIBALS

ages applied their torches to the reed fence by which the Mission House was connected with the church. And now the inmates knew that in a very few minutes the house also would be on fire, and that outside in the night armed savages would be waiting to strike them down with coward blows if they tried to make their escape.

Then it was that Mr. Paton performed a deed which, if done by a soldier on the field of battle, would be thought worthy of the Victoria Cross. Seizing a little American tomahawk with his right hand, and taking his empty revolver in the left, he issued suddenly from the door before the savages had closed in upon the house. Running towards the burning fence, he attacked that part of it which was still untouched by the fire, cutting it down with his tomahawk in a frenzy of haste, and hurling it back into the flames so that it might no longer serve as a conductor between the church and the house. At first the savages were spell-bound by his boldness, but soon several of them leaped forward with clubs uplifted. Levelling his harmless revolver at them, Mr. Paton dared them to strike him; and though they all urged one another to give the first blow, not one of them had the courage to do it.

So they stood facing each other in the lurid glow of the burning church, now flaring up through the midnight like a great torch—the intrepid white man and that band of bloodthirsty cannibals. And then there occurred something which the chief actor in this most dramatic scene has never ceased to attribute to the direct interposition of God. A rushing, roaring sound came out of the south, like the muttering of approaching thunder. Every head was turned instinctively in that direction, for the natives

JEHOVAH'S RAIN

knew by experience that a tornado was about to burst upon them.

In another moment it fell. Had it come from the north, no power on earth could have saved the Mission House and its inmates; but coming from the quarter exactly opposite, it swept the flames backwards and destroyed every chance of the house taking fire. And on the heels of the loud hurricane there came a lashing torrent of tropical rain, which before long extinguished the fire altogether. With this furious onset of the elements a panic seized the savages. "This is Jehovah's rain," they cried. And in a few moments every one of them had disappeared into the darkness, leaving Mr. Paton free to rejoin Mr. Mathieson and his wife in perfect safety.

That was Mr. Paton's last night on Tanna. Next morning the *Blue Bell*, a trading vessel, came sailing into the bay, and by it the missionaries were rescued from their now desperate situation and taken to Aneityum. Both Mr. and Mrs. Mathieson died soon after. The strain of their experiences on Tanna had been too great. But in Mr. Paton's case those years of trial and apparent defeat proved but his apprenticeship for the extraordinary work he has accomplished since.

First by his labours on the island of Aniwa, which lies between Tanna and Erromanga. The natives there, though cannibals too, were less violent and brutal than the Tannese. Dr. Paton tells how, in clearing ground to build himself a house on Aniwa, he gathered off that little spot of earth two large baskets of human bones. Pointing to them, he said to an Aniwan chief: "How do these bones come to be here?" "Ah," replied the

EPILOGUE

native, with a shrug worthy of a cynical Frenchman, "we are not Tanna men! We do not eat the bones!" The tale of Mr. Paton's life in Aniwa is as thrilling as any in the annals of the Missionary Church. But that, as Mr. Kipling would say, is another story, and cannot be told here.

Nor can we do more than allude to the romance of Mr. Paton's wanderings through the Australian bush and over the cities of England and Scotland in connexion with the building of the *Dayspring*, or rather of a succession of *Daysprings*, for shipwreck was a common thing in those coral-studded seas, and the time came besides when for mission work, as for other work, the ship of sails had to give place to the ship of steam.

And to come back to Tanna again, it can only be said that fruit appeared at length in "that hardest field in Heathendom." Dr. Paton has had the joy of seeing other men enter into his labours, the peculiar joy of giving his own son, the Rev. Frank Paton, to that same island where he toiled in loneliness and tears till driven from its shores by the savages themselves. His patient sufferings no less than his unselfish work helped to bring about at last a relenting of the Tannese heart. His early ploughshare, we might say, driven through the hard soil, opened the way for the hopeful sowers and glad reapers who came in due season.

<small>The author desires to acknowledge his special obligations to the Rev. James Paton, D.D., minister of St. Paul's Church, Glasgow, who is Dr. John G. Paton's brother and the editor of his works, for allowing him to make use of both the *Autobiography* and *The Story of John G. Paton*.</small>

CHAPTER XIII

KAPIOLANI AND THE GODDESS OF THE VOLCANO

Opukahaia at the gates of Yale—The expedition to Hawaii—Titus Coan—*New Acts of the Apostles*—An adventurous tour—Kapiolani—The march to the volcano—The pythoness of Pélé—On the floor of the crater—The challenge to the fire-goddess—Sudden fall of the Hawaiian Dagons.

ONE morning in the second decade of the nineteenth century, as some Yale students passed up the college steps on their way to their class-rooms, they found sitting at the entrance door a dark-skinned lad who was crying silently. When they asked who he was and what was wrong, he told them in his broken English a story at once strange and sad.

He was a native of the Hawaiian Islands. In one of the constant and barbarous inter-tribal fights his home had been destroyed by the victors and his father and mother cut down before his eyes. Taking his infant brother on his back, he had tried to escape, but was soon noticed, pursued, and overtaken. A ruthless spear was thrust through the body of the child he bore, while he himself was seized and dragged away into slavery.

He had gained his liberty by hiding himself on board an American ship which had called at Hawaii and was

—194—

OPUKAHAIA

homeward bound for New Haven, in Connecticut. On the long voyage round Cape Horn he was treated kindly enough, but when the vessel reached its destination he was of no use to any one, and was turned adrift to follow his own devices.

Unlike Neesima of Japan, of whom at some points his story reminds us, Opukahaia, for that was the name of this Hawaiian lad, had no Mr. Hardy waiting for him in the strange port. But as he roamed about the town, wondering what was to become of him, he came to Yale College, and saw the bands of students passing in and out. In the few words of English which he had picked up from the sailors he asked a passer-by what that great building was, and why those young men kept coming and going. He was told that this was a school of learning, and that those who entered its walls did so that wise men might teach them all that it was best to know.

Now though a Pacific islander and half a savage, Opukahaia had that same thirst for knowledge which delighted Dr. Samuel Johnson so greatly when he discovered it one day in a young waterman who was rowing him across the Thames, and which frequently appears in persons who would hardly be suspected of having any intellectual tastes at all. In this youth from Hawaii, with his dark skin and restless eyes and broken speech, there burned an eager longing to know much more than he did, and especially to learn the secret of the white man's wisdom. It seemed natural to him to turn his feet towards the College, since there, it seemed, the fountain of truth and knowledge was to be found.

But when he climbed the steps and reached the portal

AT THE GATES OF YALE

his heart had failed him utterly; and that was why the students found him crouching there that morning with the tears rolling down his cheeks.

His questioners were half-amused by this curious tale. But there were kind men among them, and many kind and Christian hearts among the good folk of the old Puritan town. An interest was awakened in Opukahaia, which led to his being provided for, and taught not only something of the wisdom of the white men, but the great saving truths of the Christian faith.

After some years had passed, Opukahaia felt that he must go back to his own islands and tell his people the good news that he had learned himself. But meanwhile the romantic story of this Hawaiian youth had become widely known, and an interest in him and his country had grown up among the American Churches. The American Board of Foreign Missions took up the matter, and decided to begin missionary work in the Hawaiian Islands. The scheme was entered into with a great deal of popular enthusiasm. And when at length in 1820 the pioneers set sail on their long voyage round the South American continent, the party included no fewer than seventeen persons besides Opukahaia himself.

In a very real sense Opukahaia may be looked upon as the founder of the American mission in Hawaii. If he had not sat weeping some years before on the doorstep of Yale College, that band of missionaries would never have sailed in the *Thaddeus* for those far-off heathen islands. But here his share in the enterprise comes to an end. He was not destined to carry the Gospel to his countrymen. The harsh New England winters had been too much for one

TITUS COAN

born amidst the soft, warm breezes of the Pacific Ocean. He died of a decline, and it was left to others to carry out that idea, which his mind had been the first to conceive, of giving to the Hawaiian people the blessings of a Christian civilization.

Beginning so romantically, the story of this American expedition grew even more romantic as time went on. Perhaps there has never been in the whole history of Protestant missions another record of such rapid and wholesale transformation of a degraded heathen race as took place in connexion with this enterprise which had been inspired by the strange vision of a Sandwich Islander knocking at the gates of a Christian college. The Rev. Titus Coan, for example, one of the leading figures of that stirring period, baptized more than 1700 persons on a single Sunday, and in one year received considerably more than 5000 men and women into the full communion of the Church. Persons who up to the time of their conversion had lived the lawless life of the savage—robbers, murderers, drunkards, the former high priests of a cruel idolatry, " their hands but recently washed from the blood of human victims "—all assembled together in Christian peace and love to partake of the sacrament of the Lord's Supper. As Dr. A. T. Pierson remarks in his *New Acts of the Apostles*, the transforming energies which swept through the islands in the early years of the Mission "find no adequate symbols but those volcanic upheavals with which the Kanakas are familiar." And yet, sudden as it was, this was no transient emotional result. It was a reconstruction of the community from its very base, "the per-

AN ADVENTUROUS TOUR

manent creation of an orderly, decorous, peaceful Christian State."

Of all the arresting incidents of this great religious revolution, the most dramatic is one which took place within the very crater of Kilauea, the largest and most awful of the active volcanoes of the world. In this dread amphitheatre, on the very brink of the eternal "Fire Fountains of Hawaii," Kapiolani, the high chieftainess of Kaavaroa, openly challenged and defied Pélé, the indwelling goddess of the volcano, as every Hawaiian believed. Her act has been likened to that of Boniface at Geismar, when with his axe he hewed down the venerable oak which had been sacred for centuries to Thor the Thunderer, while those around looked on with the fascination of horror, expecting every moment to see him struck dead by a bolt from heaven. Still more aptly the incident is compared by Miss Gordon Cumming to the great scene on Carmel, when Elijah challenged the idolatrous priests of Baal in the name of Israel's God.

In 1825 one of the missionaries, the Rev. Mr. Bishop, made a preaching tour right round the main island of Hawaii. An adventurous tour it was, for he constantly had to clamber on hands and knees up the face of precipitous cliffs, and to make his way over rugged lava beds or across deep gullies and swollen moutain torrents. At other times it was necessary to skirt the frowning rocky coast in a frail canoe, so as to circumvent those inland barriers which could not be crossed.

The native villages were often difficult to find, hidden as they were in almost inaccessible glens. But whenever this brave, adventurous preacher stood face to face with

KAPIOLANI

the people, the most wonderful results followed, and he was amply repaid for all his dangers and toils.

Among the converts of that time was Kapiolani, the most noted of all the female chiefs of Hawaii, who ruled over large possessions in the southern part of the main island. Previous to this, she had been intensely superstitious, and like most of the natives, had lived a reckless and intemperate life. Now she was utterly changed. First she set herself to reform her own life, dismissing all her husbands but one, who like herself professed Christianity, and adopting strictly sober habits. Next she did her utmost to uproot idolatrous notions and customs among her people, putting down infanticide, murder, drunkenness, and robbery with a firm hand, and without counting the possible cost to herself.

She soon realized that the great obstacle to the progress of the Gospel among the Hawaiians was their superstitious faith in the divinities of Kilauea, and above all in Pélé herself, the grim and terrible goddess who was supposed to have her dwelling-place within the crater of the burning mountain. Pélé had her retinue of priests and prophets, both male and female, whose hold upon the popular imagination was nothing short of tremendous. Their false teaching seemed to be reinforced by the great volcano with its smoking summit—an ever-present reality in the eyes of all. Its frequent eruptions revealed the might of the unseen goddess. The deep thunders of Kilauea were Pélé's own voice. The long filaments spun by the wind from the liquid lava and tossed over the edge of the crater were Pélé's dusky, streaming hair. And those priests and priestesses who offered daily sacrifice to

THE MARCH TO THE VOLCANO

her divinity were the living oracles of her will. Upon their most cruel and licentious dictates and practices there rested the sanctions of the invisible world.

Kapiolani saw quite clearly that the power of the fire-goddess must be broken before Christianity could spread in Hawaii. She accordingly resolved to challenge that power in its innermost stronghold and sanctuary, by defying Pélé to her face on the very floor of the crater of Kilauea.

When she announced her intention to her followers, they did everything they could to hold her back from such a project. Even her husband, though himself a professed Christian, begged her to abstain from a deed so rash and dangerous. But to all expostulations she had one reply. "All *tabus*," she said, "are done away. We are safe in the keeping of the Almighty God, and no power of earth or hell can harm His servants." When her people saw how determined she was they gave up trying to dissuade her, and about eighty of them were even so bold as to volunteer to accompany her to the summit of the fiery mountain.

From Kapiolani's home Kilauea was distant about one hundred miles in a straight line. To reach it was a toilsome journey—a journey which took her and her companions over jagged mountain peaks and rough lava-beds. But no détour would she make. She pressed straight on towards the volcano, over which there ever hung a dark pall of smoke by day, a lurid cloud of fire by night.

As she advanced, the people came in crowds out of the valleys to watch the progress of this strange pilgrimage. Many of them implored her to turn back ere it was too

THE PYTHONESS OF PÉLÉ

late, and not to draw down upon herself and others the vengeance of the fire-gods. But this was her invariable reply: "If I am destroyed, you may all believe in Pélé; but if I am not destroyed, you must all turn to the only true God."

At length, after a most fatiguing march, this bold champion of the new faith reached the base of Kilauea and began the upward ascent. As she approached the cone, one of Pélé's weird prophetesses appeared and warned her back in the name of the goddess. In her hand this Hawaiian pythoness held a piece of white bark-cloth, and as she waved it above her head she declared it to be a message from Pélé herself. "Read the message!" exclaimed Kapiolani. Upon which the woman held the pretended oracle before her, and poured out a flood of gibberish, which she declared to be an ancient sacred dialect. Kapiolani smiled. "You have delivered a message from your god," she said, "which none of us can understand. I too have a *pala pala*, and I will read you a message from *my* God, which every one will understand." Whereupon she opened her Hawaiian Bible and read several passages that told of Jehovah's almighty power and of the heavenly Father's saving love in Jesus Christ.

Still pressing on, Kapiolani came at length to the very edge of the vast crater, which lies one thousand feet below the summits of the enclosing cone, and led the way down the precipitous descent towards the black lava-bed. On the crater's brink there grew, like the grapes of Vesuvius, clusters of the refreshing *ohelo* berry, sacred to Pélé herself, which no Hawaiian of those days would taste till he had first cast a laden branch down the precipice towards

CHALLENGE TO FIRE-GODDESS

the fiery lake, saying as he did so: "Pélé, here are your *ohelos*. I offer some to you; some I also eat"—a formula which was supposed to render the eating safe, but without which an awful *tabu* would be infringed.

Seeing the berries hanging all around her, Kapiolani stopped and ate of them freely without making any acknowledgment to the goddess. She then made her way slowly down into the bowl of the crater, and when she reached the bottom, walked across the undulating crust of lava till she came to the *Halemaumau* itself, the "House of Everlasting Burning." Standing there, she picked up broken fragments of lava and flung them defiantly towards the seething cauldron, which writhed and moaned and flung out long hissing tongues of red and purple flame.

Having thus desecrated Pélé's holy of holies in the most dreadful manner of which a Hawaiian imagination could conceive, she now turned to her trembling followers, who stood at some distance behind, and in a loud clear voice, distinctly heard above all the deep whispers and mutterings of the volcano, she spoke these words, which were engraved for ever afterwards on the memories of all who heard them: "My God is Jehovah. He it was who kindled these fires. I do not fear Pélé. Should I perish by her wrath, then you may fear her power. But if Jehovah saves me while I am breaking her *tabus*, then you must fear and love Him. The gods of Hawaii are vain."

Kapiolani then called upon her people to kneel down on that heaving floor and offer a solemn act of adoration to the One Almighty God, and thereafter to join their

QUEEN KAPIOLANI DEFYING THE GODDESS OF THE VOLCANO

The natives of Hawaii held the goddess of the volcanic mountain of Pélé in the greatest dread. The Queen, when she became a Christian, saw that the superstition must be broken down. This she achieved by flaunting the authority of the goddess in the volcano itself, and in the presence of some of her terrified people.

FALL OF THE DAGONS

voices with hers in a hymn of joyful praise. And so by Christian praise and prayer the very crater of Kilauea, formerly the supposed abode of a cruel goddess, was consecrated as a temple to the God of holiness and love.

The news of Kapiolani's bold deed soon ran from end to end of Hawaii. It sent a shiver of despair through the hearts of Pélé's priests and votaries. Every one felt that the old dominion of the fire-gods must be tottering to its fall. Ere long the people began to turn in crowds from their idolatries. Even the heathen priests and priestesses renounced their allegiance to dark and bloody altars, and made profession of their faith in Christ.

One day a sinister figure presented itself before one of the missionaries, among a number of people who were waiting to receive some Christian instruction. It was a man whose gruesome office it had been, in the service of Pélé's altar, to hunt and catch the victims that were needed for the human sacrifices demanded by the goddess. This dreadful being had acquired the skill of a wild beast in lurking in the by-paths of the forests to leap upon the passers-by, and was possessed of such enormous strength besides that he could break the bones of his victims by simply enfolding them in his iron embrace. No wonder that on seeing him the people shrank back in terror as if from some monster of the jungle. But even this man was conquered by the gospel of love and peace, and turned from serving Pélé to follow Jesus Christ.

In the larger centres of population the natives gathered in vast multitudes to listen to the missionaries. More than once Mr. Bishop preached to assemblages that numbered upwards of ten thousand persons. Other chiefs

AN EARNEST CHIEF

and chieftainesses followed Kapiolani's example by openly professing their Christian faith. One chief showed his earnestness and zeal by building a church large enough to accommodate four thousand people. For weeks his whole tribe flung themselves joyously into the task—hewing timber in the forests, dragging it to the appointed place, cutting reeds for the thatch, and binding it carefully to the roof.

If ever there were romantic days in the history of a Christian mission, such days were experienced by those who witnessed the sudden glory of the Christian dawn that rose upon the Hawaiian Islands, flushing mountain, shore, and ocean with the radiance of the skies. There were giants and heroes, moreover, in those days; for pioneers like Mr. Bishop and Titus Coan deserve to be described by no lesser words. But so long as men tell the wonderful story of the spread of Christianity over the islands of Oceania and recall the heroes and heroines of the past, the figure of Kapiolani will stand out bravely, as she is seen in the strength of her new-born faith defying Pélé's wrath in the dark crater of Kilauea.

The story of the American Mission to Hawaii, and in particular the incident of Kapiolani's challenge to the fire-goddess, are drawn almost entirely from Miss C. F. Gordon Cumming's *Fire Fountains: The Kingdom of Hawaii* (William Blackwood and Sons), which she has generously permitted the author to make free use of for the purposes of this book.

The Mayflower Press, Plymouth, England. William Brendon & Son, Ltd.

Members of Schmul's Wesleyan Book Club buy these outstanding books at 40% off the retail price.

Join Schmul's Wesleyan Book Club by calling toll-free:

800-S$_7$P$_7$B$_2$O$_6$O$_6$K$_5$S$_7$

Put a discount Christian bookstore in your own mailbox.

Visit us on the Internet at
www.wesleyanbooks.com

You may also order direct from the publisher by writing:
Schmul Publishing Company
PO Box 776
Nicholasville, KY 40340

CPSIA information can be obtained
at www.ICGtesting.com
Printed in the USA
JSHW030847290322
24358JS00005B/326

9 780880 191043